Better Public Information for Conservationists

Government officials and major chemical companies seem willing to participate in the use of many untested substances that may irreversibly damage important areas of our world—and even damage our genetic heritage.

The general public, unable to rely on the "experts," can insist that better safeguards be used and that the relevant Government reports be made freely available to the people.

With DDT destroying bird species, and possibly damaging man himself, the wide use of herbicides that may be the precursors of almost terrifyingly potent by-products should be actively opposed.

D0199188

THE POPULATION BOMB   95¢
Dr. Paul Ehrlich

The book you can't afford not to read! Over-population is
with us now and will be the root cause of major world
problems unless it is brought under control. This book
tells what can be done—and what is likely to occur.

THE FRAIL OCEAN   95¢
Wesley Marx

"A fascinating and important book. The obvious comparison is with Rachel Carson's *Silent Spring,* and I can only
hope Mr. Marx's book will be as widely read, and have a
comparable impact."   —*New York Times*

MOMENT IN THE SUN   95¢
Robert and Leona Train Rienow

"Man's destruction of his own habitat has never been so
dramatically presented . . . a blockbuster of a book."
                              —*San Francisco Chronicle*

S/S/T AND SONIC BOOM HANDBOOK   95¢
William A. Shurcliff

A documented source book on the supersonic transport
planes (SST's) that proves the SST is an incredible, un-
necessary insult to the living environment—and tells you
what you can do to *stop the SST's.*

PERILS OF THE PEACEFUL ATOM: The Myth of Safe
    Nuclear Power Plants $1.25
Richard Curtis and Elizabeth Hogan

The case against nuclear power, a massive threat to our
world and to generations to come. "A Ralph Nader-type
book, *but the stakes are much higher* . . . should be read
by all thoughtful Americans."   —*Library Journal*

THE ENVIRONMENTAL HANDBOOK: Prepared for the First
    National Environmental Teach-In—Edited by Garrett De
    Bell   95¢
The 1970's is our last chance for a future that makes ecological sense. This handbook focuses on some of the major
problems of our deteriorating environment, explains the
nature of ecology and—most importantly—suggests action
that can be taken right now in any community, by any
individual.

To Order by mail, send price of book plus 5¢ for postage to
Dept. CS, Ballantine Books, Inc., 36 West 20th Street, New
York, New York 10003. Include your order with your address
and zip code.

DEFOLIATION
Thomas Whiteside

Foreword by George Wald

A BALLANTINE/FRIENDS OF THE EARTH BOOK

Ballantine Books, Inc. is an
INTEXT Publisher
NEW YORK

FRIENDS OF THE EARTH, founded in 1969 by David Brower, is a non-profit membership organization streamlined for aggressive political and legislative activity aimed at restoring the environment misused by man and at preserving remaining wilderness where the life force continues to flow freely.

FRIENDS OF THE EARTH is neither tax-deductible nor tax-exempt in order to fight without restrictions and invites your participation.

Addresses:

FRIENDS OF THE EARTH

30 East 42nd Street
New York, N.Y. 10017

451 Pacific Avenue
San Francisco, California 94133

917 15th Street, N.W.
Washington, D.C. 20005

1372 Kapiolani Blvd.
Honolulu, Hawaii 96814

P.O. Box 1977
Anchorage, Alaska 99501

The material on pages 1 through 53 originally appeared in *The New Yorker*, February 7 and March 14, 1970.

Copyright © 1970 by Thomas Whiteside

SBN 345-01870-2-095

First Printing: March, 1970

Printed in the United States of America

BALLANTINE BOOKS, INC.
101 Fifth Avenue, New York, N.Y. 10003

To Karen
Anne
Jimmy

Contents

Foreword

It came as an enormous relief to many Americans, in and out of the armed forces that President Nixon on November 25, 1969, renounced first, use in warfare of lethal and incapacitating weapons, all use of lethal biological agents, and ordered further production of the latter stopped and existing stockpiles destroyed. Some equivocation involving interpretation of this order and the decree to which it will be excepted must still be clarified; yet we can hope that it will go all the way.

Our country took the lead in drafting the Geneva Protocol of 1925, banning the use in war of all "asphyxiating poisonous or other gases" and of "bacteriological methods of warfare." This was signed by the United States, but not ratified by the Senate. Instead, it was allowed to die in committee. By now 84 nations, including virtually all the technologically advanced powers, have ratified or acceded to the Protocol, more than 20 since World War II; but our nation still has not ratified it. Our government has frequently declared that we accede to the terms of the Geneva Protocol, yet we are not formally bound by it.

A curious snag keeps this from happening, and clouds also President Nixon's otherwise welcome decision. We have apparently not used our most lethal CBW (Chemical and Biological weapons in actual combat—the nerve gases, the toxins, the pathogenic viruses and bacteria. We have not banned our use of so-called incapacitating gases—tear gas and CS, more a lung than a tear gas—herbicides and defoliants.

Our government and military spokesmen have been sensitive about domestic and international reaction to the use of these agents from the beginning, and from the beginning have attempted to make them seem less harmful than they are. So, for example, tear gas and CS are spoken of as "riot control" agents; and one asks, Why refuse to use on an enemy what we use on our own people? One might well question their use on our own people; but it must also be recognized that the use of such gases for riot control is altogether different from their use in combat. In riot control they are used ordinarily in the open, with the sole object of making persons move away out of the area of application. Under combat conditions these "incapacitating" gases become lethal. They are used to drive the enemy out from cover and render him helpless so that he can be destroyed with other weapons. In Vietnam CS has been used routinely to drive persons from shelter into the open before bombing and artillery attacks. Also in the bomb shelters and other closed spaces where these agents are employed they reach highly toxic concentrations. It hardly helps our case that among their victims have been many civilians.

So also with the herbicides and defoliants. One is told that they are the same agents that have been commonly used in American farms and gardens. As this book shows, the conditions of their use in Vietnam—the places they are used, the much higher concentrations, the frequency of application—all combine to turn these materials into devastating weapons.

Our government stands almost alone in exempting these agents from the terms of the Geneva Convention and insisting on continuing to use them. Apparently in the Geneva Conference of 1925 it was agreed by all that the Protocol included tear gases and herbicides among the chemical weapons it intended to ban. Philip Noel-Baker writes of a conversation he had at that time with Henri Bonnet, later Ambassador to the United States, who said, "Oh, yes; the form of words they've got is good. It prohibits every kind of chemical or bacterial weapon that anyone could possibly devise. And it has to. Perhaps some day a criminal lunatic might invent some devilish thing that would destroy animals and crops." (Letter to *New York Times*, December 9, 1969.)

As the United States Senate opened its debate on the ratification of the Geneva Protocol early in 1926, it had a letter from General John J. Pershing—Black Jack Pershing, the Commander of the American Forces in World War I—which said, "I cannot think it possible that our country should fail to ratify the Protocol which includes this or a similar provision. Scientific research may discover a gas so deadly that it will produce instant death. To sanction the use of gas in any form would be to open the way for the use of the most deadly gases and possible poisoning of whole populations of non-combatant men, women and children. The contemplation of such a result is shocking to the senses. It is unthinkable that civilization would deliberately decide upon such a course."

When President Nixon announced a few months ago that we would not use certain chemicals in war unless they are first used against us, tear gases and CS, herbicides and defoliants were exempted from the ban. On December 10, the main political committee of the General Assembly of the United Nations rejected this position decisively. Overriding vigorous opposition from the United States delegate, it voted 58 to 3 (United States, Australia and Portugal) with 35 abstentions that the Geneva Convention includes and bans "the use in international armed conflicts of any chemical agents of warfare" (*Los Angeles Times, Boston Globe,* December 11, 1969). Also on December 5, the World Health Organization condemned the use in war of defoliants and tear gases, citing the defoliants as "possible causes of birth defects in children."

Administration and Defense Department statements concerning the uses of tear gases, herbicides and defoliants in Vietnam do not rest with picturing them as relatively innocuous agents, used primarily to spare lives, including the lives of Vietnamese. They are said also to offer positive advantages at home and abroad.

So, for example, Dr. C. D. Minarik, Director of the Plant Science Laboratory at Fort Detrick, Maryland, told the Northeastern Weed Conference meeting in New York that Operation Ranch Hand, the defoliation and herbicide program in South Vietnam, not only saves lives by exposing enemy movements and hideouts, so reducing the chances of ambush, and virtually eliminating sniper fire on both troops and civilians, but that it also offers beneficial by-products to South Vietnamese civilians. They include: (a) more mangrove wood for charcoal; (b) land is cleared for eventual farming; (c) commerce is improved in isolated settlements—I suppose trading in charcoal; (d) the defoliation has uncovered Viet Cong stores of rice that can be used by the peasants for food—presumably to replace the rice we destroy and (e) improved "lines of communication" —it is easier now to get around in South Vietnam. (*Chemical and Engineering News,* Jan. 15, 1968).

By now such rhetoric is wearing thin. By the end of March, 1969, we had sprayed with defoliants over 4 million acres. Over one-fifth of the total forested area of Vietnam seems to have been defoliated at least once. In spite of prematurely optimistic reports by the Defense Department that they expect no long-term effects, it seems now that two sprayings with defoliant kill about half of the commercially valuable hardwood timber. In some mangrove areas there has been an almost total kill. It would take a generation to bring these trees back, if indeed they come back at all.

South Vietnam is a poor country. Most of its people are peasants, managing a subsistence economy through hard work on the land. The war has disrupted this frightfully. Not only has it been a quite unusually destructive war, carried out largely on an undefended countryside. Large numbers of young men for years have been taken from the farms to fight in the armies. Villages have been destroyed—bombed, burned out, bulldozed. In the free-fire zones everything that moves is fired on—people and farm animals. Enormous stretches of open rice paddies are pitted with an almost incredible density of B-52 bomb craters.

As though all that were not enough, we have engaged in a systematic program of crop destruction, said euphemistically to be directed only against the Vietcong. South Vietnam, which used to export large amounts of rice, now imports rice from the United States. Dr. Jean Mayer, Professor of Physiology and Nutrition at the Harvard School of Public Health and now President Nixon's Advisor on Nutrition, has pointed out a few years ago that though other means of warfare inevitably include civilians among their victims, crop destruction is almost exclusively directed against civilians, and indeed the most helpless civilians. The point is simple enough. When food is short, soldiers get whatever food there is. It is the unarmed, helpless and feeble that go without—the old, the ill, pregnant women, and most of all, children.

I see no way to escape the conclusion that in South Vietnam we are systematically destroying a country and its people—the very country and people that we say we are fighting to preserve. We do that with the connivance of, often at the behest of, their own government—a venal, corrupt military dictatorship that we have sponsored and to the preservation of which our present Administration is committed. People, animals, trees, crops —all are being devastated; in great stretches of open fields, that peasant families had tended by hand over many generations, the B-52 craters lie often edge to edge.

Why do we do it? The whole operation is smothered in hypocrisy, endless rhetoric, and fine language. One can get an idea of prevalent thinking from the comments of Professor Samual Huntington, who recently rotated off the Chairmanship of the Harvard Government Department, and who at the time was Chairman of the Council on Vietnamese Studies of the Southeast Asia Development Advisory Group, which advises our State Department. Professor Huntington had expressed the thought that the war was greatly speeding South Vietnamese progress in "urbanization." The evidence was that since the war began the population of Saigon had skyrocketed.

Writing in *Foreign Affairs* in July, 1968, he said: "In an absent-minded way the United States in Vietnam may well have stumbled upon the answer to 'Wars of National Liberation.' " The answer: "forced draft—urbanization and modernization which rapidly brings the country in question out of the phase in which a rural revolutionary movement can hope to generate sufficient strength to come to power." Huntington pointed out that "if the 'direct application of theoretical and conventional power' (a phrase of Sir Robert Thompson's) takes place on such a massive scale as to produce a massive migration from countryside to city, the basic assumptions underlying the Maoist doctrine of revolutionary war no longer operates. Maoist-inspired rural revolution is undercut by the American sponsored urban revolution." He went on to say that: "in the shortrun with half the population still in the country-side, the Viet Cong will remain a powerful force which cannot be dislodged from its constituency so long as the constituency continues to exist."

Apparently Professor Huntington doubts the practicality of this solution for bringing the Vietnam war to a quick end. He adds, "Peace in the immediate future must hence be based on accommodation."

It seems that whether by design or chance, the destruction of a problematical rural constituency is the program we are now engaged in. In many areas, perhaps particularly those controlled at one time or another by the National Liberation Front, every attempt has been made to drive the peasants from their homes and farms, to destroy their crops and farm animals, to deprive them of whatever stores of food they may have, and to make life so dangerous that they will move into government compounds or the cities. Senator Edward Kennedy, chairman of the Refugee Subcommittee, estimates that in the last four years there have been at least one million civilian casualties, and that at least 300,000 civilians have been killed. Even the recourse of fleeing may not be open. Orville and Jonathan Schell report that in August 1967, during Operation Benton, the "pacification" camps became so full that Army units in the field were ordered not to "generate" any more refugees. Earlier, peasants had been warned before an airstrike was called on their villages. Now they were killed in the villages, because there was no room for them in the overcrowded refugee camps (letter to *New York Times,* Nov. 26, 1969).

Just as our country was the prime mover in proposing the Geneva Protocol of 1925 banning gas and bacteriological warfare—which we still have not ratified—so our country had most to do with establishing the Nuremberg Principles, which we have formally accepted, and which are now part of International Law. Among the War Crimes are included "murder, ill-treatment or deportation—of civilian population of or in occupied territory—wanton destruction of cities, towns, or villages, or devastation not justified by military necessity." Among the Crimes Against Humanity are "inhumane acts done against any civilian population." In view of these principles, which our government accepts, this book makes strange reading.

Our present procedures in Vietnam include operations against the civilian population that come closer to genocide than to the waging of war as Americans have understood it in the past, as generally accepted by civilized nations and embodied in International Law. The wide and indiscriminate use of tear gases, herbicides and defoliants looms large among those procedures.

Taken together with the free-fire zones, the kill ratio, the body count, they add up to an orgy of destruction that is new in American military history. War has been called the pursuit of diplomacy by other—to be sure violent—means. But this is total war in the pure; it spares nothing, not even the trees, not even the earth and water. It has reduced war to an engineering problem, to an exercise in the unbridled technology of destruction, that goes with and feeds our present military economy—our business of death, now the principal business in America, the biggest business in the world, the biggest business in human history.

These practices are not only destroying a small and poor country and people thousands of miles away. They are destroying the American tradition, and all that it has meant to us and to the world.

These practices must stop. The use of tear gases, herbicides and defoliants in Vietnam and in all future wars can be stopped easily. All that is needed is for our Government to agree with almost all other civilized nations that the ban on chemical and biological weapons of war that we already accept in principle includes these weapons also.

GEORGE WALD
Cambridge, Mass.
March 15, 1970

DEFOLIATION

LATE in 1961, the United States Military Advisory Group in Vietnam began, as a minor test operation, the defoliation, by aerial spraying, of trees along the sides of roads and canals east of Saigon. The purpose of the operation was to increase visibility and thus safeguard against ambushes of allied troops and make more vulnerable any Vietcong who might be concealed under cover of the dense foliage. The number of acres sprayed does not appear to have been publicly recorded, but the test was adjudged a success militarily. In January, 1962, following a formal announcement by South Vietnamese and American officials that a program of such spraying was to be put into effect, and that it was intended "to improve the country's economy by permitting freer communication as well as to facilitate the Vietnamese Army's task of keeping these avenues free of Vietcong harassments," military defoliation operations really got under way. According to an article that month in the New York *Times*, "a high South Vietnamese official" announced that a seventy-mile stretch of road between Saigon and the coast was sprayed "to remove foliage hiding Communist guerrillas." The South Vietnamese spokesman also announced that defoliant chemicals would be sprayed on Vietcong plantations of manioc and sweet potatoes in the Highlands. The program was gathering momentum. It was doing so in spite of certain private misgivings among American officials, particularly in the State Department, who feared, first, that the operations might open the United States to charges of engaging in chemical and biological warfare, and, second, that they were not all that militarily effective. Roger Hilsman, now a professor of government at Columbia University, and then Director of Intelligence and Research for the State Department, reported, after a trip to Vietnam, that defoliation operations "had political disadvantages" and, furthermore, that they were of questionable military value, particularly in accomplishing their supposed purpose of reducing cover for ambushes. Hilsman later recalled in his book, "To Move a Nation," his visit to Vietnam, in March, 1962: "I had flown down a stretch of road that had been used for a test and found that the results were not very impressive. . . . Later, the senior Australian military representative in Saigon, Colonel Serong, also pointed out that defoliation actually aided the ambushers—if the vegetation was close to the road those who were ambushed could take cover quickly; when it was removed the guerrillas had a better field of fire." According to Hilsman, "The National Security Council spent tense sessions debating the matter."

Nonetheless, the Joint Chiefs of Staff and their Chairman, General Maxwell Taylor, agreed that chemical defoliation was a useful military weapon. In 1962, the American military "treated" 4,940 acres of the Vietnamese countryside with herbicides. In 1963, the area sprayed increased five-fold, to a total of 24,700 acres. In 1964, the defoliated area was more than tripled. In 1965, the 1964 figure was doubled, increasing to 155,-610 acres. In 1966, the sprayed area was again increased fivefold, to 741,247 acres, and in 1967 it was doubled once again over the previous year, to 1,486,446 acres. Thus, the areas defoliated in Vietnam had increased approximately three hundred-fold in five years, but now adverse opinion among scientists and other people who were concerned about the effects of defoliation on the Vietnamese ecology at last began to have a braking effect on the program. In 1968, 1,267,110 acres were sprayed, and in 1969 perhaps a million acres. Since 1962, the defoliation operations have covered almost five million acres, an area equivalent to about twelve per cent of the entire territory of South Vietnam, and about the size of the state of Massachusetts. Between 1962 and 1967, the deliberate destruction of plots of rice, manioc, beans, and other foodstuffs through herbicidal spraying—the word "deliberate" is used here to exclude the many reported instances of accidental spraying of Vietnamese plots—increased three hundredfold, from an estimated 741 acres to 221,312 acres, and by the end of 1969 the Vietnamese crop-growing area that since 1962 had been sprayed with herbicides totalled at least half a million acres. By then, in many areas the original purpose of the defoliation had been all but forgotten. The military had discovered that a more effective way of keeping roadsides clear was to bulldoze them. But by the time of that discovery defoliation had settled in as a general policy and taken on a life of its own—mainly justified on the ground that it made enemy infiltration from the North much more difficult by removing vegetation that concealed jungle roads and trails.

During all the time since the program began in 1961, no American military or civilian official has ever publicly characterized it as an operation of either chemical or biological warfare, although there can be no doubt that it is an operation of chemical warfare in that it involves the aerial spraying of chemical substances with the aim of gaining a military advantage, and that it is an operation of biological warfare in that it is aimed at a deliberate disruption of the biological conditions prevailing in a given area. Such distinctions simply do not appear in official United States statements or documents; they were long ago shrouded under heavy verbal cover. Thus, a State Department report, made public in March, 1966, saying that about twenty thousand acres of crops in South Vietnam had been destroyed by defoliation to deny food to guerrillas, described the areas involved as "remote and thinly populated," and gave a firm assurance that the materials sprayed on the crops were of a mild and transient potency: "The herbicides used are non-toxic and not dangerous to man or animal life. The land is not affected for future use."

HOWEVER comforting the statements issued by our government during seven years of herbicidal operations in Vietnam, the fact is that the major development of defoliant chemicals (whose existence had been known in the thirties) and other herbicidal agents came about in military programs for biological warfare. The direction of this work was set during the Second World War, when Professor E. J. Kraus, who then headed the Botany Department of the University of Chicago, brought certain scientific possibilities to the attention of a committee that had been set up by Henry L. Stimson, the Secretary of War, under the National Research Council, to provide the military with advice on various aspects of biological warfare. Kraus, referring to the existence of hormone-like substances that experimentation had shown would kill certain plants or disrupt their growth, suggested to the committee in 1941 that it might be interested in "the toxic properties of growth-regulating substances for the destruction of crops or the limitation of crop production." Military research on herbicides thereupon got under way, principally at Camp (later Fort) Detrick, Maryland, the Army center for biological-warfare research. According to George Merck, a chemist, who headed Stimson's biological-warfare advisory committee,

"Only the rapid ending of the war prevented field trials in an active theatre of synthetic agents that would, without injury to human or animal life, affect the growing crops and make them useless."

After the war, many of the herbicidal materials that had been developed and tested for biological-warfare use were marketed for civilian purposes and used by farmers and homeowners for killing weeds and controlling brush. The most powerful of the herbicides were the two chemicals 2,4-dichlorophenoxyacetic acid, generally known as 2,4-D, and 2,4,5-trichlorophenoxyacetic acid, known as 2,4,5-T. The direct toxicity levels of these chemicals as they affected experimental animals, and, by scientific estimates, men, appeared then to be low (although these estimates have later been challenged), and the United States Department of Agriculture, the Food and Drug Administration, and the Fish and Wildlife Service all sanctioned the widespread sale and use of both. The chemicals were also reported to be short-lived in soil after their application. 2,4-D was the bigger seller of the two, partly because it was cheaper, and suburbanites commonly used mixtures containing 2,4-D on their lawns to control dandelions and other weeds. Commercially, 2,4-D and 2,4,5-T were used to clear railroad rights-of-way and power-line routes, and, in cattle country, to get rid of woody brush, 2,4,5-T being favored for the last, because it was considered to have a more effective herbicidal action on woody plants. Very often, however, the two chemicals were used in combination. Between 1945 and 1963, the production of herbicides jumped from nine hundred and seventeen thousand pounds to about a hundred and fifty million pounds in this country; since 1963, their use has risen two hundred and seventy-one per cent—more than double the rate of increase in the use of pesticides, though pesticides are still far more extensively used. By 1960, an area equivalent to more than three per cent of the entire United States was being sprayed each year with herbicides.

Considering the rapidly growing civilian use of these products, it is perhaps not surprising that the defoliation operations in Vietnam escaped any significant comment in the press, and that the American public remained un- aware of the extent to which these uses had their origin in planning for chemical and biological warfare. Nevertheless, between 1941 and the present, testing and experimentation in the use of 2,4-D, 2,4,5-T, and other herbicides as military weapons were going forward very actively at Fort Detrick. While homeowners were using herbicidal mixtures to keep their lawns free of weeds, the military were screening some twelve hundred compounds for their usefulness in biological-warfare operations. The most promising of these compounds were test-sprayed on tropical vegetation in Puerto Rico and Thailand, and by the time full-scale defoliation operations got under way in Vietnam the U.S. military had settled on the use of four herbicidal spray materials there. These went under the names Agent Orange, Agent Purple, Agent White, and Agent Blue—designations derived from color-coded stripes girdling the shipping drums of each type of material. Of these materials, Agent Orange, the most widely used as a general defoliant, consists of a fifty-fifty mixture of n butyl esters of 2,4-D and 2,4,5-T. Agent Purple, which is interchangeable with Agent Orange, consists of the same substances with slight molecular variations. Agent White, which is used mostly for forest defoliation, is a combination of 2,4-D and Picloram, produced by the Dow Chemical Company. Unlike 2,4-D or 2,4,5-T, which, after application, is said to be decomposable by microorganisms in soil over a period of weeks or months (one field test of 2,4,5-T in this country showed that significant quantities persisted in soil for ninety-three days after application), Picloram—whose use the Department of Agriculture has not authorized in the cultivation of any American crop—is one of the most persistent herbicides known. Dr. Arthur W. Galston, professor of biology at Yale, has described Picloram as "a herbicidal analog of DDT," and an article in a Dow Chemical Company publication called "Down to Earth" reported that in field trials of Picloram in various California soils between eighty and ninety-six and a half per cent of the substance remained in the soils four hundred and sixty-seven days after application. (The rate at which Picloram decomposes in tropical soils may, however, be higher.) Agent Blue consists of a solution of cacodylic acid, a substance that contains fifty-four per cent arsenic, and it is used in Vietnam to destroy rice crops. According to the authoritative "Merck Index," a source book on chemicals, this material is "poisonous." It can be used on agricultural crops in this country only under certain restrictions imposed by the Department of Agriculture. It is being used herbicidally on Vietnamese rice fields at seven and a half times the concentration permitted for weed-killing purposes in this country, and so far in Vietnam something like five thousand tons is estimated to have been sprayed on paddies and vegetable fields.

Defoliation operations in Vietnam are carried out by a special flight of the 12th Air Commando Squadron of the United States Air Force, from a base at Bien Hoa, just outside Saigon, with specially equipped C-123 cargo planes. Each of these aircraft has been fitted out with tanks capable of holding a thousand gallons. On defoliation missions, the herbicide carried in these tanks is sprayed from an altitude of around a hundred and fifty feet, under pressure, from thirty-six nozzles on the wings and tail of the plane, and usually several spray planes work in formation, laying down broad blankets of spray.

The normal crew of a military herbicidal-spray plane consists of a pilot, a co-pilot, and a technician, who sits in the tail area and operates a console regulating the spray. The equipment is calibrated to spray a thousand gallons of herbicidal mixture at a rate that works out, when all goes well, to about three gallons per acre. Spraying a thousand-gallon tankload takes five minutes. In an emergency, the tank can be emptied in thirty seconds—a fact that has particular significance because of what has recently been learned about the nature of at least one of the herbicidal substances.

The official code name for the program is Operation Hades, but a more friendly code name, Operation Ranch Hand, is commonly used. In similar fashion, military public-relations men refer to the herbicidal spraying of crops supposedly grown for Vietcong use in Vietnam, when they refer to it at all, as a "food-denial program." By contrast, an American biologist who is less than enthusiastic about the effort has called it, in its current phase, "escalation to a program of starvation of the population in the affected area." Dr. Jean Mayer, the Harvard professor who now is President Nixon's special adviser on nutrition, contended in an article in *Science and Citizen* in 1967 that the ultimate target of herbicidal operations against rice and other crops in Vietnam was "the weakest element of the civilian population"—that is, women, children, and the elderly—because in the sprayed areas "Vietcong soldiers may . . . be expected to get the fighter's share of whatever food there is." He pointed out that malnutrition is endemic in many parts of Southeast Asia but that in wartime South Vietnam, where diseases associated with malnutrition, such as beriberi, anemia, kwashiorkor (the disease that has decimated the Biafran population), and tuberculosis, are particularly widespread, "there can be no doubt that if the [crop-destruction] program is continued, [the] problems will grow."

WHETHER a particular mission involves defoliation or crop destruction, American military spokesmen insist that a mission never takes place without careful consideration of all the factors involved, including the welfare of friendly inhabitants and the safety of American personnel. (There can be little doubt that defoliation missions are extremely hazardous to the members of the planes' crews, for the planes are required to fly very low and only slightly above stalling speed, and they are often targets of automatic-weapons fire from the ground.) The process of setting up targets and approving specific herbicidal operations is theoretically subject to elaborate review through two parallel chains of command: one chain consisting of South Vietnamese district and province chiefs—who can themselves initiate such missions—and South Vietnamese Army commanders at various levels; the other a United States chain, consisting of a district adviser, a sector adviser, a divisional senior adviser, a corps senior adviser, the United States Military Assistance Command in South Vietnam, and the American Embassy in Saigon, ending up with the American ambassador himself. Positive justification of the military advantage likely to be gained from each operation is theoretically required, and applications without such positive justification are theoretically disapproved. However, according to one of a series of articles by Elizabeth Pond that appeared toward the end of 1967 in the *Christian Science Monitor*:

In practice, [American] corps advisers find it very difficult to turn down defoliation requests from province level because they simply do not have sufficient specific knowledge to call a proposed operation into question.

And with the momentum of six years' use of defoliants, the practice, in the words of one source, has long since been "set in cement."

The real burden of proof has long since shifted from the positive one of justifying an operation by its [military] gains to the negative one of denying an operation because of [specific] drawbacks. There is thus a great deal of pressure, especially above province level, to approve recommendations sent up from below as a matter of course.

Miss Pond reported that American military sources in Saigon were "enthusiastic" about the defoliation program, and that American commanders and spotter-plane pilots were "clamoring for more of the same." She was given firm assurances as to the mild nature of the chemicals used in the spray operations:

> The defoliants used, according to the military spokesman contacted, are the same herbicides . . . as those used commercially over some four million acres in the United States. In the strengths used in Vietnam they are not at all harmful to humans or animals, the spokesman pointed out, and in illustration of this he dabbed onto his tongue a bit of liquid from one of . . . three bottles sitting on his desk.

As the apparently inexorable advance of defoliation operations in South Vietnam continued, a number of scientists in the United States began to protest the military use of herbicides, contending that Vietnam was being used, in effect, as a proving ground for chemical and biological warfare. Early in 1966, a group of twenty-nine scientists, under the leadership of Dr. John Edsall, a professor of biochemistry at Harvard, appealed to President Johnson to prohibit the use of defoliants and crop-destroying herbicides, and called the use of these substances in Vietnam "barbarous because they are indiscriminate." In the late summer of 1966, this protest was followed by a letter of petition to President Johnson from twenty-two scientists, including seven Nobel laureates. The petition pointed out that the "large-scale use of anticrop and 'non-lethal' antipersonnel chemical weapons in Vietnam" constituted "a dangerous precedent" in chemical and biological warfare, and it asked the President to order it stopped. Before the end of that year, Dr. Edsall and Dr. Matthew S. Meselson, a Harvard professor of biology, obtained the signatures of five thousand scientists to co-sponsor the petition. Despite these protests, the area covered by defoliation operations in Vietnam in 1967 was double that covered in 1966, and the acreage of crops destroyed was nearly doubled.

These figures relate only to areas that were sprayed intentionally. There is no known way of spraying an area with herbicides from the air in a really accurate manner, because the material used is so highly volatile, especially under tropical conditions, that even light wind drift can cause extensive damage to foliage and crops outside the deliberately sprayed area. Crops are so sensitive to the herbicidal spray that it can cause damage to fields and gardens as much as fifteen miles away from the target zone. Particularly severe accidental damage is reported, from time to time, to so-called "friendly" crops in the III Corps area, which all but surrounds Saigon and extends in a rough square from the coastline to the Cambodian border. Most of the spraying in III Corps is now done in War Zones C and D, which are classified as free fire zones, where, as one American official has put it, "everything that moves in Zones C and D is considered Charlie." A press dispatch from Saigon in 1967 quoted another American official as saying that every Vietnamese farmer in that corps area knew of the defoliation program and disapproved of it. Dr. Galston, the

Yale biologist, who is one of the most persistent critics of American policy concerning herbicidal operations in Vietnam, recently said in an interview, "We know that most of the truck crops grown along roads, canals, and trails and formerly brought into Saigon have been essentially abandoned because of the deliberate or inadvertent falling of these defoliant sprays; many crops in the Saigon area are simply not being harvested." He also cited reports that in some instances in which the inhabitants of Vietnamese villages have been suspected of being Vietcong sympathizers the destruction of food crops has brought about complete abandonment of the villages. In 1966, herbicidal operations caused extensive inadvertent damage, through wind drift, to a very large rubber plantation northwest of Saigon owned by the Michelin rubber interests. As the result of claims made for this damage, the South Vietnamese authorities paid the corporate owners, through the American military, nearly a million dollars. The extent of the known inadvertent damage to crops in Vietnam can be inferred from the South Vietnamese budget—in reality, the American military budget—for settling such claims. In 1967, the budget for this compensation was three million six hundred thousand dollars. This sum, however, probably reflects only the barest emergency claims of the people affected.

According to Representative Richard D. McCarthy, a Democrat from upstate New York who has been a strong critic of the program, the policy of allowing applications for defoliation operations to flow, usually without question, from the level of the South Vietnamese provincial or district chiefs has meant that these local functionaries would order repeated sprayings of areas that they had not visited in months, or even years. The thought that a Vietnamese district chief can initiate such wholesale spraying, in effect without much likelihood of serious hindrance by American military advisers, is a disquieting one to a number of biologists. Something that disquiets many of them even more is what they believe the long-range effects of nine years of defoliation operations will be on the ecology of South Vietnam. Dr. Galston, testifying recently before a congressional subcommittee on chemical and biological warfare, made these observations:

It has already been well documented that some kinds of plant associations subject to spray, especially by Agent Orange, containing 2,4-D and 2,4,5-T, have been irreversibly damaged. I refer specifically to the mangrove associations that line the estuaries, especially around the Saigon River. Up to a hundred thousand acres of these mangroves have been sprayed. . . . Some [mangrove areas] had been sprayed as early as 1961 and have shown no substantial signs of recovery. . . . Ecologists have known for a long time that the mangroves lining estuaries furnish one of the most important ecological niches for the completion of the life cycle of certain shellfish and migratory fish. If these plant communities are not in a healthy state, secondary effects on the whole interlocked web of organisms are bound to occur. . . . In the years ahead the Vietnamese, who do not have overabundant sources of proteins anyhow, are probably going to suffer dietarily because of the deprivation of food in the form of fish and shellfish.

Damage to the soil is another possible consequence of extensive defoliation. . . . We know that the soil is not a dead, inert mass but, rather, that it is a vibrant, living community. . . . If you knock the leaves off of trees once, twice, or three times . . . you change the quality of the soil. . . . Certain tropical soils—and it has been estimated that in Vietnam up to fifty per cent of all the soils fall into this category—are lateralizable; that is, they may be irreversibly converted to rock as a result of the deprivation of organic matter. . . . If . . . you deprive trees of leaves and photosynthesis stops, organic matter in the soil declines and laterization, the making of brick, may occur on a very extensive scale. I would emphasize that this brick is irreversibly hardened; it can't be made back into soil. . . .

Another ecological consequence is the invasion of an area by undesirable plants. One of the main plants that invade an area that has been defoliated is bamboo. Bamboo is one of the most difficult of all plants to destroy once it becomes established where you don't want it. It is not amenable to killing by herbicides. Frequently it has to be burned over, and this causes tremendous dislocations to agriculture.

Dr. Fred H. Tschirley, assistant chief of the Crops Protection Research Branch of the Department of Agriculture, who made a month's visit to Vietnam in the spring of 1968 in behalf of the State Department to report on the ecological effects of herbicidal operations there, does not agree with Dr. Galston's view that laterization of the soil is a serious probability. However, he reported to the State Department that in the Rung Sat area, southeast of Saigon, where about a hundred thousand acres of mangrove trees had been sprayed with defoliant, each single application of Agent Orange had killed ninety to a hundred per cent of the mangroves touched by the spray, and he estimated that the regeneration of the mangroves in this area would take another twenty years, at least. Dr. Tschirley agrees with Dr. Galston that a biological danger attending the defoliation of mangroves is an invasion of virtually ineradicable bamboo.

A fairly well-documented example not only of the ecological consequences of defoliation operations but also of their disruptive effects on human life was provided last year by a rubber-plantation area in Kompong Cham Province, Cambodia, which lies just across the border from Vietnam's Tay Ninh Province. On June 2, 1969, the Cambodian government, in an angry diplomatic note to the United States government, charged the United States with major defoliation damage to rubber plantations, and also to farm and garden crops in the province, through herbicidal operations deliberately conducted on Cambodian soil. It demanded compensation of eight and a half million dollars for destruction or serious damage to twenty-four thousand acres of trees and crops. After some delay, the State Department conceded that the alleged damage might be connected with "accidental drift" of spray over the border from herbicidal operations in Tay Ninh Province. The Defense Department flatly denied that the Cambodian areas had been deliberately sprayed. Late in June, the State Department sent a team of four American scientists to Cambodia, and they confirmed the extent of the area of damage that the Cambodians had claimed. They found that although some evidence of spray drift across the Vietnamese border existed, the extent and severity of damage in the area worst affected were such that "it is highly unlikely that this quantity could have drifted over from the Tay Ninh defoliation operations." Their report added, "The evidence we have seen, though circumstantial, suggests strongly that damage was caused by direct overflight." A second report on herbicidal damage to the area was made after an unofficial party of American biologists, including Professor E. W. Pfeiffer, of the University of Montana, and Professor Arthur H. Westing, of Windham College, Vermont, visited Cambodia last December at the invitation of the Cambodian government. They found that about a third of all the rubber trees currently in production in Cambodia had been damaged, and this had happened in an area that normally had the highest latex yield per acre of any in the world. A high proportion of two varieties of rubber trees in the area had died as a result of the damage, and Dr. Westing estimated that the damage to the latex-producing capacity of some varieties might persist for twenty years. Between May and November of last year, latex production in the affected plantations fell off by an average of between thirty-five and forty per cent. According to a report by the two scientists, "A large variety of garden crops were devastated in the seemingly endless number of small villages scattered thoughout the affected area. Virtually all of the . . . local inhabitants . . . depend for their well-being upon their own local produce. These people saw their crops . . . literally wither before their eyes." The Cambodian claim is still pending.

UNTIL the end of last year, the criticism by biologists of the dangers involved in the use of herbicides centered on their use in what were increasingly construed as biological-warfare operations, and on the disruptive effects of these chemicals upon civilian populations and upon the ecology of the regions in which they were used. Last year, however, certain biologists began to raise serious questions on another score—possible direct hazards to life from 2,4,5-T. On October 29th, as a result of these questions, a statement was publicly issued by Dr. Lee DuBridge, President Nixon's science adviser. In summary, the statement said that because a laboratory study of mice and rats that had been given relatively high oral doses of 2,4,5-T in early stages of pregnancy "showed a higher than expected number of deformities" in the offspring, the government would, as a precautionary measure, undertake a series of coördinated actions to restrict the use of 2,4,5-T in both domestic civilian applications and military herbicidal operations. The DuBridge statement identified the laboratory study as having been made by an organization called the Bionet-

ics Research Laboratories in Bethesda, Maryland, but
gave no details of either the findings or the data on
which they were based. This absence of specific information turned out to be characteristic of what has been
made available to the public concerning this particular
research project. From the beginning, it seems, there
was an extraordinary reluctance to discuss details of
the purported ill effects of 2,4,5-T on animals. Six weeks
after the publication of the DuBridge statement, a jour-
nalist who was attempting to obtain a copy of the full
report made by Bionetics and to discuss its details with
some of the government officials concerned encountered
hard going. At the Bionetics Laboratories, an official
said that he couldn't talk about the study, because "we're
under wraps to the National Institutes of Health"—the
government agency that commissioned the study. Then,
having been asked what the specific doses of 2,4,5-T
were that were said to have increased birth defects in the
fetuses of experimental animals, the Bionetics official cut
off discussion by saying, "You're asking sophisticated
questions that as a layman you don't have the equipment
to understand the answers to." At the National Institutes
of Health, an official who was asked for details of or a
copy of the study on 2,4,5-T replied, "The position I'm
in is that I have been requested not to distribute this information." He did say, however, that a continuing
evaluation of the study was under way at the National
Institute of Environmental Health Sciences, at Research
Triangle Park, North Carolina. A telephone call to an
officer of this organization brought a response whose
tone varied from wariness to downright hostility and
made it clear that the official had no intention of discuss-
ing details or results of the study with the press.

The Bionetics study on 2,4,5-T was part of a series
carried out under contract to the National Cancer Institute, which is an arm of the National Institutes of Health,

to investigate more than two hundred compounds, most of them pesticides, in order to determine whether they induced cancer-causing changes, fetus-deforming changes, or mutation-causing changes in experimental animals. The contract was a large one, involving more than two and a half million dollars' worth of research, and its primary purpose was to screen out suspicious-looking substances for further study. The first visible fruits of the Bionetics research were presented in March of last year before a convention of the American Association for the Advancement of Science, in the form of a study of possible carcinogenic properties of the fifty-three compounds; the findings on 2,4,5-T were that it did not appear to cause carcinogenic changes in the animals studied.

By the time the report on the carcinogenic properties of the substances was presented, the results of another part of the Bionetics studies, concerning the teratogenic, or fetus-deforming, properties of the substances, were being compiled, but these results were not immediately made available to biologists outside the government. The data remained—somewhat frustratingly, in the view of some scientists who had been most curious about the effects of herbicides—out of sight, and a number of attempts by biologists who had heard about the teratological study of 2,4,5-T to get at its findings appear to have been thwarted by the authorities involved. Upon being asked to account for the apparent delay in making this information available to biologists, an official of the National Institute of Environmental Health Sciences (another branch of the National Institutes of Health) has declared, with some heat, that the results of the study itself and of a statistical summary of the findings prepared by the Institute were in fact passed on as they were completed to the Commission on Pesticides and Their Relationship to Environmental Health, a scientific group appointed by Secretary of Health, Education, and Welfare Robert Finch and known—after its chairman, Dr. E. M. Mrak, of the University of California—as the Mrak Commission. Dr. Samuel S. Epstein, chief of the Laboratories of Environmental Toxicology and Carcinogenesis at the Children's Cancer Research Foundation in Boston, who was co-chairman of the Mrak Commission panel considering the teratogenic potential of pesticides, tells a different story on the availability of the Bionetics study. He says that he first heard about it in February. At a meeting of his panel in August, he asked for a copy of the report. Ten days later, the panel was told that the National Institute of Environmental Health Sciences would be willing to provide a statistical summary but that the group could not have access to the full report on which the summary was based. Dr. Epstein says that the panel eventually got the full report on September 24th "by pulling teeth."

Actually, as far back as February, officials at the National Cancer Institute had known, on the basis of a preliminary written outline from Bionetics, the findings of the Bionetics scientists on the fetus-deforming role of 2,4,5-T. Dr. Richard Bates, the officer of the National Institutes of Health who was in charge of coördinating the Bionetics project, has said that during the same month this information was put into the hands of officials of the Food and Drug Administration, the Department of Agriculture, and the Department of Defense. "We had a meeting with a couple of scientists from Fort Detrick, and we informed them of what we had learned," Dr. Bates said recently. "I don't know whether they were the right people for us to see. We didn't hear from them again until after the DuBridge announcement at the White House. Then they called up and asked for a copy of the Bionetics report."

At the Department of Agriculture, which Dr. Bates

said had been informed in February of the preliminary Bionetics findings, Dr. Tschirley, one of the officials most intimately concerned with the permissible uses of herbicidal compounds, says that he first heard about the report on 2,4,5-T through the DuBridge announcement. At the Food and Drug Administration, where appropriate officials had been informed in February of the teratogenic potential of 2,4,5-T, no new action was taken to safeguard the public against 2,4,5-T in foodstuffs. In fact, it appears that no action at all was taken by the Food and Drug Administration on the matter during the whole of last year. The explanation that F.D.A. officials have offered for this inaction is that they were under instructions to leave the whole question alone at least until December, because the matter was under definitive study by the Mrak Commission—the very group whose members, as it turns out, had such extraordinary difficulty in obtaining the Bionetics data. The Food Toxicology Branch of the F.D.A. did not have access to the full Bionetics report on 2,4,5-T until after Dr. DuBridge issued his statement, at the end of October.

Thus, after the first word went to various agencies about the fetus-deforming potential of 2,4,5-T, and warning lights could have flashed on in every branch of the government and in the headquarters of every company manufacturing or handling it, literally almost nothing was done by the officials charged with protecting the public from exposure to dangerous or potentially dangerous materials—by the officials in the F.D.A., in the Department of Agriculture, and in the Department of Defense. It is conceivable that the Bionetics findings might still be hidden from the public if they had not been pried loose in midsummer through the activities of a group of young law students. The students were members of a team put together by the consumer-protection activist Ralph Nader—and often referred to as Nader's Raiders—to explore the labyrinthine workings of the Food and Drug Administration. In the course of their investigations, one of the law students, a young woman named Anita Johnson, happened to see a copy of the preliminary report on the Bionetics findings that had been passed on to the F.D.A. in February, and its observations seemed quite disturbing to her. Miss Johnson wrote a report to Nader, and in September she showed a copy of the report to a friend who was a biology student at Harvard. In early October, Miss Johnson's friend, in a conversation with Professor Matthew Meselson, mentioned Miss Johnson's report on the preliminary Bionetics findings. This was the first that Dr. Meselson had heard of the existence of the Bionetics study. A few days previously, he had received a call from a scientist friend of his asking whether Dr. Meselson had heard of certain stories, originating with South Vietnamese journalists and other South Vietnamese, of an unusual incidence of birth defects in South Vietnam, which were alleged to be connected with defoliation operations there.

A few days later, after his friend sent him further information, Dr. Meselson decided to obtain a copy of the Bionetics report, and he called up an acquaintance in a government agency and asked for it. He was told that the report was "confidential and classified," and inaccessible to outsiders. Actually, in addition to the preliminary report there were now in existence the full Bionetics report and a statistical summary prepared by the National Institute of Environmental Health Sciences, and, by nagging various Washington friends, Dr. Meselson obtained bootlegged copies of the two latest reports. What he read seemed to him to have such serious implications that he got in touch with acquaintances in the White House and also with someone in the Army to alert them to the problems of 2,4,5-T, in the hope that some new restrictions would be placed on its use. According to Dr. Meselson, the White House people apparently didn't know until that moment that the reports on the adverse effects of 2,4,5-T even existed. (Around that time, according to a member of Nader's Raiders, "a tremendous lid was put on this thing" within government agencies, and on the subject of the Bionetics work and 2,4,5-T "people in government whom we'd been talking to freely for years just shut up and wouldn't say a word.") While Dr. Meselson awaited word on the matter, a colleague of his informed the press about the findings of the Bionetics report. Very shortly thereafter, Dr. DuBridge made his public announcement of the proposed restrictions on the use of 2,4,5-T.

IN certain respects, the DuBridge announcement is a curious document. In its approach to the facts about 2,4,5-T that were set forth in the Bionetics report, it reflects considerable sensitivity to the political and international issues that lie behind the widespread use of this powerful herbicide for civilian and military purposes, and the words in which it describes the reasons for restricting its use appear to have been very carefully chosen:

> The actions to control the use of the chemical were taken as a result of findings from a laboratory study conducted by Bionetics Research Laboratories which indicated that offspring of mice and rats given relatively large oral doses of the herbicide during early stages of pregnancy showed a higher than expected number of deformities.
>
> Although it seems improbable that any person could receive harmful amounts of this chemical from any of the existing uses of 2,4,5-T, and while the relationships of these effects in laboratory animals to effects in man

are not entirely clear at this time, the actions taken will assure safety of the public while further evidence is being sought.

These actions, according to the statement, included decisions that the Department of Agriculture would cancel manufacturers' registrations of 2,4,5-T for use on food crops, effective at the beginning of 1970, "unless by that time the Food and Drug Administration has found a basis for establishing a safe legal tolerance in and on foods," and that the Departments of Agriculture and the Interior, in their own programs, would stop the use of 2,4,5-T in populated areas and in all other areas where residues of the substance could reach man. As for military uses of 2,4,5-T, the statement said, "The chemical is effective in defoliating trees and shrubs and its use in South Vietnam has resulted in reducing greatly the number of ambushes, thus saving lives." However, the statement continued, "the Department of Defense will [henceforth] restrict the use of 2,4,5-T to areas remote from the population."

All this sounds eminently fair and sensible, but whether it represents a candid exposition of the facts about 2,4,5-T and the Bionetics report is debatable. The White House statement that the Bionetics findings "indicated that offspring of mice and rats given relatively large oral doses of the herbicide during early stages of pregnancy showed a higher than expected number of deformities" is, in the words of one eminent biologist who has studied the Bionetics data, "an understatement." He went on to say that "if the effects on experimental animals are applicable to people it's a very sad and serious situation." The actual Bionetics report described 2,4,5-T as producing "sufficiently prominent effects of seriously hazardous nature" in controlled experiments with pregnant mice to lead the authors "to

categorize [it] as *probably dangerous.*" The report also
found 2,4-D "potentially dangerous but needing further
study." As for 2,4,5-T, the report noted that, with the
exception of very small subcutaneous dosages, "all
dosages, routes, and strains resulted in increased incidence of abnormal fetuses" after its administration. The
abnormalities in the fetuses included lack of eyes, faulty
eyes, cystic kidneys, cleft palates, and enlarged livers.
The Bionetics report went on to report on further experimental applications of 2,4,5-T to another species:

> Because of the potential importance of the findings in
> mice, an additional study was carried out in rats of the
> Sprague-Dawley strain. Using dosages of 21.5 and 46.4
> mg/kg [that is, dosages scaled to represent 21.5 and 46.4
> milligrams of 2,4,5-T per kilogram of the experimental
> animal's body weight] suspended in 50 per cent honey
> and given by the oral route on the 6th through 15th days
> of gestation, we observed excessive fetal mortality
> (almost 80 per cent) and a high incidence of abnormal-
> ities in the survivors. When the beginning of administra-
> tion was delayed until the 10th day, fetal mortality was
> somewhat less but still quite high even when dosage was
> reduced to 4.6 mg/kg. The incidence of abnormal fetuses
> was threefold that in controls even with the smallest
> dosage and shortest period used. . . .
> It seems inescapable that 2,4,5-T is teratogenic in this
> strain of rats when given orally at the dosage schedules
> used here.

Considering the fetus-deforming effects of the *lowest*
oral dosage of 2,4,5-T used in the Bionetics work on rats
—to say nothing of the excessive fetal mortality—the
White House statement that "relatively large oral doses
of the herbicide . . . showed a higher than expected number of deformities" is hardly an accurate description of
the results of the study. In fact, the statistical tables
presented as part of the Bionetics report showed that at

the lowest oral dosage of 2,4,5-T given to pregnant rats between the tenth and fifteenth days of gestation thirty-nine per cent of the fetuses produced were abnormal, or three times the figure for control animals. At what could without much question be described as "relatively large oral doses" of the herbicide—dosages of 21.5 and 46.4 milligrams per kilogram of body weight of rats, for example—the percentage of abnormal fetuses was ninety and a hundred per cent, respectively, or a good bit higher than one would be likely to deduce from the phrase "a higher than expected number of deformities." The assertion that "it seems improbable that any person could receive harmful amounts of this chemical from any of the existing uses of 2,4,5-T" also appears to be worth examining, for this is precisely what many biologists are most worried about in relation to 2,4,5-T and allied substances.

It seems fair, before going further, to quote a cautionary note in the DuBridge statement: "The study involved relatively small numbers of laboratory rats and mice. More extensive studies are needed and will be undertaken. At best it is difficult to extrapolate results obtained with laboratory animals to man—sensitivity to a given compound may be different in man than in animal species. . . ." It would be difficult to get a biologist to disagree with these seemingly sound generalities. However, the first part of the statement does imply, at least to a layman, that the number of experimental animals used in the Bionetics study had been considerably smaller than the numbers used to test commercial compounds other than 2,4,5-T before they are approved by agencies such as the Food and Drug Administration and the Department of Agriculture. In this connection, the curious layman could reasonably begin with the recommendations, in 1963, of the President's Science Advisory Committee on the use of pesticides, which proposed that companies putting out pesticides should be required from then on to demonstrate the safety of their products by means of toxicity studies on two generations of at least two warm-blooded mammalian species. Subsequently, the F.D.A. set up new testing requirements, based on these recommendations, for companies producing pesticides. However, according to Dr. Joseph McLaughlin, of the Food Toxicology Branch of the F.D.A., the organization actually requires applicants for permission to sell pesticides to present the results of tests on only *one* species (usually, in practice, the rat). According to Dr. McLaughlin, the average number of experimental animals used in studies of pesticides is between eighty and a hundred and sixty, including animals used as controls but excluding litters produced. The Bionetics studies of 2,4,5-T used both mice and rats, and their total number was, in fact, greater, not less, than this average. Including controls but excluding litters, the total number of animals used in the 2,4,5-T studies was two hundred and twenty-five. Analysis of the results by the National Institute of Environmental Health Sciences found them statistically "significant," and this is the real purpose of such a study: it is meant to act as a coarse screen to shake out of the data the larger lumps of bad news. Such a study is usually incapable of shaking out anything smaller; another kind of study is needed to do that.

Thus, the DuBridge statement seems to give rise to this question: If the Bionetics study, based on the effects of 2,4,5-T on two hundred and twenty-five experimental animals of two species, appears to be less than conclusive, on the ground that "the study involved relatively small numbers of laboratory rats and mice," what is one to think of the adequacy of the tests that the manufacturers of pesticides make? If, as the DuBridge statement says, "at best it is difficult to extrapolate results obtained with laboratory animals to man," what is one to say of the protection that the government affords the consumer when the results of tests of pesticidal substances on perhaps a hundred and twenty rats are officially extrapolated to justify the use of the substances by a population of two hundred million people—not to mention one to two million unborn babies being carried in their mothers' wombs?

The very coarseness of the screen used in all these tests—that is, the relatively small number of animals involved—means that the bad news that shows up in the data has to be taken with particular seriousness, because lesser effects tend not to be demonstrable at all. The inadequacy of the scale on which animal tests with, for instance, pesticides are currently being made in this country to gain F.D.A. approval is further indicated by the fact that a fetus-deforming effect that might show up if a thousand test animals were used is almost never picked up, since the studies are not conducted on that scale; yet if the material being tested turned out to have the same effect, quantitatively, on human beings, this would mean that it would cause between three and four thousand malformed babies to be produced each year. The teratogenic effects of 2,4,5-T on experimental animals used by the Bionetics people, however, were not on the order of one in a thousand. Even in the case of the lowest oral dose given rats, they were on the order of one in three.

Again, it is fair to say that what is applicable to rats in such tests may not be applicable to human beings. But it is also fair to say that studies involving rats are conducted not for the welfare of the rat kingdom but for the ultimate protection of human beings. In the opinion of Dr. Epstein, the fact that the 2,4,5-T used in the Bionetics study produced teratogenic effects in *both* mice and rats underlines the seriousness of the study's implications. In the opinion of Dr. McLaughlin, this is even further underlined by another circumstance—that the rat, as a test animal, tends to be relatively resistant to teratogenic effects of chemicals. For example, in the late nineteen-fifties, when thalidomide, that disastrously teratogenic compound, was being tested on rats in oral dosages ranging from low to very high, no discernible fetus-deforming effects were produced. And Dr. McLaughlin says that as far as thalidomide tests on rabbits were concerned, "You could give thalidomide to rabbits in oral doses at between fifty and two hundred times the comparable human level to show any comparable teratogenic effects." In babies born to women who took thalidomide, whether in small or large dosages and whether in single or multiple dosages, between the sixth and seventh weeks of pregnancy, the rate of deformation was estimated to be one in ten.

Because of the relatively coarse testing screen through which compounds like pesticides—and food additives as well—are sifted before they are approved for general or specialized use in this country, the Food and Drug Administration theoretically maintains a policy of stipulating, as a safety factor, that the maximum amount of such a substance allowable in the human diet range from one two-thousandth to one one-hundredth of the highest dosage level of the substance that produces no harmful effects in experimental animals. (In the case of pesticides, the World Health Organization takes a more conservative view, considering one two-thousandth of the "no-effect" level in animal studies to be a reasonable safety level for human exposure.) According to the standards of safety established by F.D.A. policy then, no human being anywhere should ever have been exposed to 2,4,5-T, because in the Bionetics study of rats *every* dosage level produced deformed fetuses. A "no-effect" level was never achieved.

To make a reasonable guess about the general safety of 2,4,5-T for human beings, as the material has been used up to now, the most appropriate population area to observe is probably not the relatively healthy and well-fed United States, where human beings are perhaps better equipped to withstand the assault of toxic substances, but South Vietnam, where great numbers of civilians are half-starved, ravaged by disease, and racked by the innumerable horrors of war. In considering any potentially harmful effects of 2,4,5-T on human beings in Vietnam, some attempt has to be made to estimate the amount of 2,4,5-T to which people, and particularly pregnant women, may have been exposed as a result of the repeated defoliation operations. To do so, a comparison of known rates of application of 2,4,5-T in the United States and in Vietnam is in order. In this country, according to Dr. Tschirley, the average recommended application of 2,4,5-T in aerial spraying for woody-plant control is between three-quarters of a pound and a pound per acre. There are about five manufacturers of 2,4,5-T in this country, of which the Dow Chemical Company is one of the biggest. One of Dow Chemical's best-sellers in the 2,4,5-T line is Esteron 245 Concentrate, and the cautionary notes that a drum of Esteron bears on its label are hardly reassuring to anyone lulled by prior allegations that 2,4,5-T is a substance of low toxicity:

CAUTION—
MAY CAUSE SKIN IRRITATION
Avoid Contact with Eyes, Skin,
and Clothing
Keep out of the reach of children

Under the word "WARNING" are a number of instructions concerning safe use of the material, and these include, presumably for good reason, the following admonition:

> Do not contaminate irrigation ditches or water used for domestic purposes.

Then comes a "NOTICE":

> Seller makes no warranty of any kind, express or implied, concerning the use of this product. Buyer assumes all risk of use or handling, whether in accordance with directions or not.

The concentration of Esteron recommended—subject to all these warnings, cautions, and disclaimers—for aerial spraying in the United States varies with the type of vegetation to be sprayed, but probably a fair average would be three-quarters to one pound acid equivalent of the raw 2,4,5-T per acre. In Vietnam, however, the concentration of 2,4,5-T for each acre sprayed has been far higher. In Agent Orange, the concentrations of 2,4,5-T have averaged *thirteen times* the recommended concentrations used in the United States. The principal route through which quantities of 2,4,5-T might be expected to enter the human system in Vietnam is through drinking water, and in the areas sprayed most drinking water comes either from rainwater cisterns fed from house roofs or from very shallow wells. It has been calculated that, taking into account the average amount of 2,4,5-T in Agent Orange sprayed per acre in Vietnam by the military, and assuming a one-inch rainfall (which is quite common in South Vietnam) after a spraying, a forty-kilo (about eighty-eight-pound) Vietnamese woman drinking two litres (about 1.8 quarts) of contaminated water a day could very well be absorbing into her system a hundred and twenty milligrams, or about one two-hundred-and-fiftieth of an ounce, of 2,4,5-T a day; that is, a daily oral dosage of three milligrams of 2,4,5-T per kilo of body weight. Thus, if a Vietnamese woman who was exposed to Agent Orange was pregnant, she might very well be absorbing into her system a percentage of 2,4,5-T only slightly less than the percentage that deformed one out of every three fetuses of the pregnant experimental rats. To pursue further the question of exposure of Vietnamese to 2,4,5-T concentrations in relation to concentrations officially considered safe for Americans, an advisory subcommittee to the Secretary of the Interior, in setting up guidelines for maximum safe contamination of surface water by pesticides and allied substances some time ago, recommended a concentration of one-tenth of a milligram of 2,4,5-T in one litre of drinking water as the maximum safe concentration. Thus, a pregnant Vietnamese woman who ingested a hundred and twenty milligrams of 2,4,5-T in two litres of water a day would be exposed to 2,4,5-T at six hundred times the concentration officially considered safe for Americans.

Moreover, the level of exposure of Vietnamese people in sprayed areas is not necessarily limited to the concentrations shown in Dr. Meselson's calculations. Sometimes the level may be far higher. Dr. Pfeiffer, the University of Montana biologist, says that when difficulties arise with the spray planes or the spray apparatus, or when other accidents occur, an entire thousand-gallon load of herbicidal agent containing 2,4,5-T may be dumped in one area by means of the thirty-second emergency-dumping procedure. Dr. Pfeiffer has recalled going along as an observer on a United States defoliation mission last March, over the Plain of Reeds area of Vietnam, near the Cambodian border, during which the technician at the spray controls was unable to get the apparatus to work, and thereupon dumped his whole load. "This rained down a dose of 2,4,5-T that must have been fantastically concentrated," Dr. Pfeiffer has said. "It was released on a very watery spot that looked like headwaters draining into the Mekong River, which hundreds of thousands of people use." In another instance, he has recalled, a pilot going over the area of the supposedly "friendly" Catholic refugee village of Ho Nai, near Bien Hoa, had serious engine trouble and dumped his whole spray load of herbicide on or near the village. In such instances, the concentration of 2,4,5-T dumped upon an inhabited area in Vietnam probably averaged about a hundred and thirty times the concentration recommended by 2,4,5-T manufacturers as both effective and safe for use in the United States.

THEORETICALLY, the dangers inherent in the use of 2,4,5-T should have been removed by means of the steps promised in the White House announcement last October. A quick reading of the statement by Dr. Du-Bridge (who is also the executive secretary of the President's Environmental Quality Council) certainly seemed to convey the impression that from that day onward there would be a change in Department of Defense policy on the use of 2,4,5-T in Vietnam, just as there would be a change in the policies of the Departments of Agriculture and the Interior on the domestic use of 2,4,5-T. But did the White House mean what it certainly seemed to be saying about the future military use of 2,4,5-T in Vietnam? The White House statement was issued on October 29th. On October 30th, the Pentagon announced that no change would be made in the policy governing the military use of 2,4,5-T in South Vietnam, because—so the Washington *Post* reported on October 31st—"the Defense Department feels its present policy conforms to the new Presidential directive." The *Post* article went on:

A Pentagon spokesman's explanation of the policy, read at a morning press briefing, differed markedly from the written version given reporters later.

When the written statement was distributed, reporters were told not to use the spokesman's [previous] comment that the defoliant . . . is used against enemy "training and regroupment centers."

The statement was expunged after a reporter asked how use against such centers conformed to the Defense Department's stated policy of prohibiting its use in "populated areas."

But the statement wasn't so easily expunged. A short time later, it was made again, in essence, by Rear Admiral William E. Lemos, of the Policy Plans and National Security Council Affairs Office of the Department of Defense, in testimony before a subcommittee of the House Foreign Affairs Committee, the only difference being that the phrase "training and regroupment centers" became "enemy base camps." And in testifying that the military was mounting herbicidal operations on alleged enemy base camps Rear Admiral Lemos said:

We know . . . that the enemy will move from areas that have been sprayed. Therefore, enemy base camps or unit headquarters are sprayed in order to make him move to avoid exposing himself to aerial observation.

If one adds to the words "enemy base camps" the expunged words "training and regroupment centers"—centers that are unlikely to operate without an accompanying civilian population—what the Defense Department seems actually to be indicating is that the "areas remote from the population" against which the United States is conducting military herbicidal operations are "remote from the population" at least in part *because* of these operations.

As for the Bionetics findings on the teratogenic effects of 2,4,5-T on experimental animals, the Department of Defense indicated that it put little stock in the dangers suggested by the report. A reporter for the *Yale Daily News* who telephoned the Pentagon during the first week in December to inquire about the Defense Department's attitude toward its use of 2,4,5-T in the light of the Bionetics report was assured that "there is no cause for alarm about defoliants." A week or so later, he received a letter from the Directorate for Defense Information at the Pentagon which described the Bionetics results as based on "evidence that 2,4,5-T, when fed in large amounts to highly inbred and susceptible mice and rats, gave a higher incidence of birth defects than was normal for these animals." After reading this letter, the *Yale Daily News* reporter again telephoned the Pentagon, and asked, "Does [the Department of Defense] think defoliants could be affecting embryo growth in any way in Vietnam?" The Pentagon spokesman said, "No." And that was that. The experimental animals were highly susceptible; the civilian Vietnamese population, which even under "normal" circumstances is the victim of a statistically incalculable but clearly very high abortion and infant-mortality rate, was not.

NEARLY a month after Dr. DuBridge's statement, another was issued, this one by the President himself, on United States policy on chemical and biological warfare. The President, noting that "biological weapons have massive, unpredictable, and potentially uncontrollable consequences" that might "impair the health of future generations," announced it as his decision that thenceforward "the United States shall renounce the use of lethal biological agents and weapons, and all other methods of biological warfare." Later, a White House spokesman, in answer to questions by reporters whether this included the use of herbicidal, defoliant, or crop-killing chemicals in Vietnam, made it clear that the new policy did not encompass herbicides.

Since the President's statement did specifically renounce "all other methods of biological warfare," the reasonable assumption is that the United States government does not consider herbicidal, defoliant, and crop-killing operations against military and civilian populations to be part of biological warfare. The question therefore remains: What does the United States government consider biological warfare to consist of? The best place to look for an authoritative definition is a work known as the Joint Chiefs of Staff Dictionary, an official publication that governs proper word usage within the military establishment. In the current edition of the Joint Chiefs of Staff Dictionary, "biological warfare" is defined as the "employment of living organisms, toxic biological products, and plant-growth regulators to produce death or casualties in man, animals, or plants or defense against such action." But the term "plant-growth regulators" is nowhere defined in the Joint Chiefs of Staff Dictionary, and since a certain technical distinction might be made (by weed-control scientists, for example) between plant-growth regulators and defoliants, the question of whether the Joint Chiefs consider military defoliation operations part of biological warfare is left unclear. As for "defoliant agents," the Dictionary defines such an agent only as "a chemical which causes trees, shrubs, and other plants to shed their leaves prematurely." All this is hardly a surprise to anyone familiar with the fast semantic legerdemain involved in all official statements on biological warfare, in which defoliation has the bafflingly evanescent half-existence of a pea under a shell.

To find that pea in the official literature is not easy. But it is reasonable to assume that if the Department of

Defense were to concede officially that "defoliant agents" were in the same category as "plant-growth regulators" that "produce death . . . in plants," it would thereby also be conceding that it is in fact engaging in the biological warfare that President Nixon has renounced. And such a concession seems to have been run to earth in the current edition of a Department of the Army publication entitled "Manual on Use of Herbicides for Military Purposes," in which "antiplant agents" are defined as "chemical agents which possess a high offensive potential for destroying or seriously limiting the production of food and defoliating vegetation," and goes on, "These compounds include herbicides that kill or inhibit the growth of plants; plant-growth regulators that either regulate or inhibit plant growth, sometimes causing plant death. . . ." The admission that the Department of Defense is indeed engaging, through its defoliation and herbicidal operations in Vietnam, in biological warfare, as this is defined by the Joint Chiefs and as it has been formally renounced by the President, seems inescapable.

SINCE the DuBridge statement, allegations, apparently originating in part with the Dow Chemical Company, have been made to the effect that the 2,4,5-T used in the Bionetics study was unrepresentative of the 2,4,5-T generally produced in this country, in that it contained comparatively large amounts of a certain contaminant, which, according to the Dow people, is ordinarily present in 2,4,5-T only in trace quantities. Accordingly, it has been suggested that the real cause of the teratogenic effects of the 2,4,5-T used in the Bionetics study may not have been the 2,4,5-T itself but, rather, the contaminant in the sample used. The chemical name of the contaminant thus suspected by the Dow people is 2,3,6,7-tetrachlorodibenzo-p-dioxin, often referred to simply as

dioxin. The 2,4,5-T used by Bionetics was obtained in
1965 from the Diamond Alkali Company, now known
as the Diamond-Shamrock Company and no longer in
the business of manufacturing 2,4,5-T. It appears that
the presence of a dioxin contaminant in the process of
manufacturing 2,4,5-T is a constant problem among all
manufacturers. Three years ago, Dow was obliged to
close down its 2,4,5-T plant in Midland, Michigan, for
several months and partly rebuild it because of what
Dow people variously described as "a problem" and
"an accident." The problem—or accident—was that
workers exposed to the dioxin contaminant during the
process of manufacture came down with an acute skin
irritation known as chloracne. The Dow people, who
speak with considerable pride of their toxicological work
("We established our toxicology lab the year Ralph
Nader was born," a Dow public-relations man said recently, showing, at any rate, that Dow is keenly aware of
Nader and his career), say that the chloracne problem
has long since been cleared up, and that the current level
of the dioxin contaminant in Dow's 2,4,5-T is less than
one part per million, as opposed to the dioxin level in
the 2,4,5-T used in the Bionetics study, which is alleged
to have been between fifteen and thirty parts per million.
A scientist at the DuBridge office, which has become a
coördinating agency for information having to do with
the 2,4,5-T question, says that the 2,4,5-T used by Bionetics was "probably representative" of 2,4,5-T being
used in this country—and presumably in Vietnam—at
the time it was obtained but that considerably less of the
contaminant is present in the 2,4,5-T now being produced. Evidently, the degree of dioxin contamination
present in 2,4,5-T varies from manufacturer to manufacturer. What degree of contamination, high or low, was
present in the quantities of 2,4,5-T shipped to South

Vietnam at various times this spokesman didn't seem to know.

The point about the dioxin contamination of 2,4,5-T is an extremely important one, because if the suspicions of the Dow people are correct and the cause of the fetus deformities cited in the Bionetics study is not the 2,4,5-T but the dioxin contaminant, then this contaminant may be among the most teratogenically powerful agents ever known. Dr. McLaughlin has calculated that if the dioxin present in the Bionetics 2,4,5-T was indeed responsible for the teratogenic effects on the experimental animals, it looks as though the contaminant would have to be at least ten thousand times more teratogenically active in rats than thalidomide was found to be in rabbits. Furthermore, it raises alarming questions about the prevalence of the dioxin material in our environment. It appears that under high heat the dioxin material can be produced in a whole class of chemical substances known as trichlorophenols and pentachlorophenols. These substances include components of certain fatty acids used in detergents and in animal feed.

As a consequence of studies that have been made of the deaths of millions of young chicks in this country after the chicks had eaten certain kinds of chicken feed, government scientists are now seriously speculating on the possibility that the deaths were at the end of a chain that began with the spraying of corn crops with 2,4,5-T. The hypothesis is that residues of dioxin present in the 2,4,5-T remained in the harvested corn and were concentrated into certain by-products that were then sold to manufacturers of chicken feed, and that the dioxin became absorbed into the systems of the young chicks. One particularly disquieting sign of the potential of the dioxin material is the fact that bio-assays made on chick embryos in another study revealed that all the embryos were killed by one twenty-millionth of a gram of dioxin per egg.

Perhaps an even more disquieting speculation 'about the dioxin is that 2,4,5-T may not be the only material in which it appears. Among the compounds that several experienced biologists and toxicologists suspect might contain or produce dioxin are the trichlorophenols and pentachlorophenols, which are rather widely present in the environment in various forms. For example, a number of the trichlorophenols and pentachlorophenols are used as slime-killing agents in paper-pulp manufacture, and are present in a wide range of consumer products, including adhesives, water-based and oil-based paints, varnishes and lacquers, and paper and paper coatings. They are used to prevent slime in pasteurizers and fungus on vats in breweries and are also used in hair shampoo. Along with the 2,4,5-T used in the Bionetics study, one trichlorophenol and one pentachlorophenol were tested without teratogenic results. But Dr. McLaughlin points out that since there are many such compounds put out by various companies, these particular samples might turn out to be—by the reasoning of the allegation that the 2,4,5-T used by Bionetics was unusually dirty—unusually clean.

Dr. McLaughlin tends to consider significant, in view of the now known extreme toxicity and possible extreme teratogenicity of dioxin, the existence of even very small amounts of the trichlorophenols and pentachlorophenols in food wrappings and other consumer products. Since the production of dioxin appears to be associated with high-temperature conditions, a question arises whether these thermal conditions are met at *any* stage of production or subsequent use or disposal of such materials, even in minute amounts. One of the problems here seems to be, as Dr. Epstein has put it, "The moment you introduce something into the environment it's likely to be burned sooner or later—that's the way we get rid of nearly everything." And most of these consumer products may wind up in municipal incinerators, and when they are burned, the thermal and other conditions for creating dioxin materials may quite possibly be met. If so, this could mean a release of dioxin material into the entire environment through the atmosphere.

Yet so far the dioxin material now suspected of causing the fetus-deforming effects in experimental animals has never been put through any formal teratological tests by any company or any government agency. If the speculation over the connection between dioxin in 2,4,5-T and the deaths of millions of baby chicks is borne out, it might mean that, quite contrary to the assumptions made up to now that 2,4,5-T is rapidly decomposable in soil, the dioxin material may be extremely persistent as well as extremely deadly.

So far, nobody knows—and it is probable that nobody will know for some time—whether the fetus deformities in the Bionetics study were caused by the 2,4,5-T itself, by the dioxin contaminant, or by some other substance or substances present in the 2,4,5-T, or whether human fetuses react to 2,4,5-T in the same way as the fetuses of the experimental animals in the Bionetics study. However, the experience so far with the employment of 2,4,5-T and substances chemically allied to it ought to be instructive. The history of 2,4,5-T is related to preparations for biological warfare, although nobody in the United States government seems to want to admit this, and it has wound up being used for purposes of biological warfare, although nobody in the United States government seems to want to admit *this,* either. Since 2,4,5-T was developed, the United States government has allowed it to be used on a very large scale on our

own fields and countryside without adequate tests of
its effects. In South Vietnam—a nation we are attempting to save—for seven full years the American military
has sprayed or dumped this biological-warfare material
on the countryside, on villages, and on South Vietnamese
men and women in staggering amounts. In that time, the
military has sprayed or dumped on Vietnam *fifty thousand tons* of herbicide, of which twenty thousand tons
have apparently been straight 2,4,5-T. In addition, the
American military has apparently made incursions into a
neutral country, Cambodia, and rained down on an area
inhabited by thirty thousand civilians a vast quantity of
2,4,5-T. Yet in the quarter of a century since the Department of Defense first developed the biological-
warfare uses of this material it has not completed a single
series of formal teratological tests on pregnant animals
to determine whether it has an effect on their unborn
offspring.

Similarly, officials of the Dow Chemical Company,
one of the largest producers of 2,4,5-T, although they
refuse to divulge how much 2,4,5-T they are and have
been producing, admit that in all the years that they
had produced the chemical before the DuBridge statement they had never made formal teratological tests on
their 2,4,5-T, which they are now doing. The Monsanto
Chemical Company, another big producer, had, as far
as is known, never made such tests, either, nor, according to an official in the White House, had any other
manufacturer. The Department of Agriculture has never
required any such tests from manufacturers. The Food
and Drug Administration has never required any such
tests from manufacturers. The first tests to determine
the teratogenic effects of 2,4,5-T were not made until
the National Institutes of Health contracted for them
with Bionetics Laboratories. And even then, when the

adverse results of the tests became apparent, it was, as Dr. Epstein said, like "pulling teeth" to get the data out of the institutions involved. And when the data were obtained and the White House was obliged, partly by outside pressure and publicity, to act, the President's science adviser publicly presented the facts in a less than candid manner, while the Department of Defense, for all practical purposes, ignored the whole business and announced its intention of going on doing what it had been doing all along.

There have been a number of reports from Vietnam both of animal abortions and of malformed human babies that are thought to have resulted from spraying operations in which 2,4,5-T was used. But such scattered reports, however well founded, cannot really shed much more light on the situation. The fact is that even in this country, the best-fed, richest, and certainly most statistics-minded of all countries on earth, the standards for testing materials that are put into the environment, into drugs, and into the human diet are grossly inadequate. The screening system is so coarse that, as a teratology panel of the Mrak Commission warned recently, in connection with thalidomide, "the teratogenicity of thalidomide might have been missed had it not produced malformations rarely encountered." In other words, had it not been for the fact that very unusual and particularly terrible malformations appeared in an obvious pattern—for example, similarly malformed babies in the same hospital at about the same time—pregnant women might still be using thalidomide, and lesser deformations would, so to speak, disappear into the general statistical background. As for more subtle effects, such as brain damage and damage to the central nervous system, they would probably never show up as such at all. If such risks existed under orderly, normal medical conditions in a highly developed country, how is one ever to measure the harm that might be done to unborn children in rural Vietnam, in the midst of the malnutrition, the disease, the trauma, the poverty, and the general shambles of war?

Further Observations
on 2,4,5-T

The Editors, *The New Yorker,*
DEAR SIRS:

IN an article that appeared in *The New Yorker* on
February 7th, I wrote that Dr. Lee DuBridge, the President's science adviser, issued a statement last October
at the White House saying that because a laboratory
study had shown a "higher than expected number of
deformities" in the fetuses of mice and rats exposed to
the herbicide 2,4,5-T, agencies of the United States
government would take action to restrict the use of that
substance in this country and in Vietnam, where it was
being used in extensive military defoliation operations.
This action, Dr. DuBridge announced, would include
the cancellation, by January 1st of this year, of Department of Agriculture permits for the use of 2,4,5-T on
some American food crops unless the Food and Drug
Administration had by then been able to determine a
safe concentration of the herbicide in foods. Dr.
DuBridge further announced that the Department of
Defense would thenceforth "restrict the use of 2,4,5-T
to areas remote from the population" in Vietnam. His
statement added that these actions and others "will

assure the safety of the public while further evidence [of the alleged harmful effects of 2,4,5-T] is being sought."

Four months have passed, and 2,4,5-T is still being used as widely as ever. The Department of Agriculture has yet to cancel its permits for the use of the herbicide on food crops in this country, and the Department of Defense is continuing to use it in populated areas of Vietnam. In the meantime, officials of the Dow Chemical Company, which is one of the largest producers of 2,4,5-T, have been maintaining that the samples of 2,4,5-T used in the study cited by Dr. DuBridge, which was done by the Bionetics Research Laboratories, of Bethesda, Maryland, were uncharacteristic of the 2,4,5-T currently being produced, because the material tested by Bionetics—which did not come from Dow—was contaminated to an unusual extent by a toxic substance identified as symmetrical 2,3,6,7-tetrachlorodibenzo-p-dioxin. This contaminant, usually called dioxin, was alleged by the Dow people to be present in the Bionetics samples at a concentration of approximately twenty-seven parts per million, and they claim that the 2,4,5-T that Dow is currently producing contains the dioxin contaminant in concentrations of less than one part per million. The Dow people maintain that their currently produced 2,4,5-T does not appear to have the effect of deforming rat fetuses. In January, a Dow official told the Department of Health, Education, and Welfare, "We strongly urge that action concerning the status of 2,4,5-T be held in abeyance until [Dow's] testing program is completed [in] April." The United States government's failure so far to place the promised restrictions on the use of 2,4,5-T in this country may in part be attributed to this plea.

Because of the seriousness of the issues involved, it seems to me that the government's failure to act on the use of 2,4,5-T here and in Vietnam calls for much fuller public discussion. Even though the dioxin contaminant may now be present in 2,4,5-T in what the Dow Chemical Company apparently considers to be no more than tolerable amounts, the substance is of such potency that its release even in small concentrations must prompt deep concern. In the presumably more heavily dioxin-contaminated samples of 2,4,5-T that were used in the Bionetics work, the smallest dosages of 2,4,5-T that the test animals were given caused extensive deformities in fetuses. In more recent studies of the dioxin contaminant, conducted by Dr. Jacqueline Verrett, of the Food and Drug Administration (who earlier was responsible for revealing the carcinogenicity of cyclamates), extensive teratogenic, or fetus-deforming, effects were discovered in chick embryos when the dioxin, or a distillate predominantly consisting of it, was present at concentrations of little more than a trillionth of a gram per gram of the egg. The magnitude of this effect on chick embryos may be gathered from the fact that, according to Dr. Verrett's studies, the dioxin appears to be a million times as potent a fetus-deforming agent as the notorious teratogen thalidomide was found to be in tests on chicks. Of course, chick embryos are far down the biological ladder from human fetuses, and they are also extremely sensitive to many substances. But even if, for theoretical purposes, we reduced the teratogenic power of the dioxin, as shown in Dr. Verrett's chick-embryo studies, approximately a million times, we would *still* have to consider that we were dealing with a substance as teratogenically potent as thalidomide. That the United States government permits the presence, even in minute amounts, of such a substance in herbicidal mixtures to be sold for spraying on food crops and on suburban lawns—where some of the chemical may enter shallow wells and other drinking-water supplies—is hardly reassuring. And it is particularly disturbing when one reflects that in the quarter of a century in which 2,4,5-T was used prior to Dr. DuBridge's announcement not a single regulatory agency of the United States government, not the Department of Defense—which has been spreading huge quantities of 2,4,5-T on vast areas of Vietnam—and not, as far as is known, the researchers for any one of the half-dozen large American chemical companies producing the material had ever so much as opened up a pregnant mouse to determine whether 2,4,5-T or the dioxin contaminant in it did any systemic or pathogenic harm to the fetus. Several studies of the sort are now under way, but the United States government still seems to take the position that the 2,4,5-T produced by Dow and other large chemical companies should be considered innocent until it is proved to be otherwise. Meanwhile, 2,4,5-T is being sprayed on certain crops and on areas where it may come into contact with human beings, cattle, and wildlife. In Vietnam, it is still being sprayed by the military in concentrations that average thirteen times as great as those that the manufacturers themselves recommend as safe and effective for use in this country.

It is true that the teratogenicity of dioxin—as distinct from dioxin-contaminated 2,4,5-T—has not yet been established in tests conducted on experimental animals of mammalian species. However, the direct toxic, or body-poisoning, effects—as distinct from fetus-deforming effects—of dioxin are known to be very high both in animals and in human beings. In past studies on rats, dosages of forty-five millionths of a gram per kilo of the mother's body weight have been found to kill fifty per cent of the offspring. When dioxin was given orally to pregnant rats in recent tests, it was found, on preliminary investigation, to kill all fetuses with dosages of eight millionths of a gram per kilo of the mother's body weight, and to damage fetuses with dosages of a half-millionth of a gram per kilo.

Further, the effects of dioxin on human beings, even in small dosages, are known to be serious. In the past, in plants manufacturing 2,4,5-T an illness called chloracne seems to have been widespread among the workers. In the mid-sixties, Dow was obliged to close down part of a 2,4,5-T plant in Midland, Michigan, for some time because about sixty workers contracted chloracne as a result of contact with dioxin, which seems to be always present in varying degrees during the process of manufacturing 2,4,5-T and in the finished 2,4,5-T itself. The symptoms of this disease include extensive skin eruptions, disorders of the central nervous system, chronic fatigue, lassitude, and depression. Workers at a 2,4,5-T plant in New Jersey run by another company suffered similar symptoms in the mid-sixties, and six years later some of them were reported to be still suffering from the effects of the disease. In Germany, since the mid-fifties, workers in factory after factory producing 2,4,5-T and polychlorophenolic compounds have been afflicted with chloracne after absorbing apparently only minute amounts of the dioxin contaminant; their symptoms have been described in several medical papers as including liver damage, nervous and mental disorders, depression, loss of appetite and weight, and markedly reduced sexual drive.

A FEW weeks ago, when a reporter approached an official in Dr. DuBridge's office for information on 2,4,5-T he was told that he would be given White House coöperation "only to a certain extent," because the official didn't want "wild speculation" stirred up. He cited as an example of "wild speculation" the recent controversy over the birth-control pill, which, he said, had "caused millions of women to get hysterical with worry." The reporter replied that he didn't think the analogy between 2,4,5-T and the Pill was a particularly good one, for the reason that a woman using the Pill could employ alternative methods of contraception, whereas a Vietnamese woman exposed to herbicidal spray put down by the American military had no choice in the matter.

But perhaps the comparison between 2,4,5-T (and its dioxin contaminant) and commonly used pills is worth pursuing. Suppose that such a dangerous substance as dioxin were found to be contained in a pill offered for human consumption in this country, and suppose that the contaminant were present in such minute amounts that an adult following the prescribed dosages might ingest a hundredth of a millionth of a gram of the contaminant per day. There is no doubt whatever that, according to existing Food and Drug Administration standards, the F.D.A. would immediately ban production and sale of the pill on the ground that it was highly dangerous to public health; in fact, the amount of such a potent contaminant that the F.D.A. would permit in a pill under the agency's present policy on toxicity would almost certainly be zero.

While 2,4,5-T, with or without the dioxin contaminant, doesn't come in pill form, it may be worthwhile to try to calculate, on the basis of a hypothetical pill, how much 2,4,5-T (and dioxin) a Vietnamese woman living in an area sprayed by the American military might ingest in a day. It has already been calculated by reputable biologists that, if one takes into account the average amount of 2,4,5-T sprayed per acre in Vietnam, and also takes into account a one-inch rainfall—such as is common there—after a spraying, a forty-kilo (about eighty-eight-pound) Vietnamese woman drinking two litres (about two quarts) of 2,4,5-T-contaminated water per day could be ingesting about a hundred and twenty milligrams (about a two-hundred-and-fiftieth of an ounce) of 2,4,5-T a day. If the 2,4,5-T contained the dioxin contaminant at a level of one part per million—which is what the Dow people say is the maximum amount present in the 2,4,5-T they are currently producing—the Vietnamese woman would be absorbing a little over a tenth of a microgram of dioxin per day, or ten times the amount of dioxin entering the system of an adult from the hypothetical pill that the F.D.A. would certainly find dangerous to human health. Further, if this Vietnamese woman were to conceive a child two weeks, say, after the spraying, the weight of the dioxin that by these same calculations would have then accumulated in her system (the evidence thus far is that dioxin accumulates in mammalian tissue in the same manner as the chlorinated hydrocarbons, such as DDT) would be more than the weight of the just-fertilized ovum. Considering the existing evidence of the frightening degree of teratogenicity of the dioxin in chick embryos and its highly toxic effects on mammalian fetuses, the presence of this much dioxin in a mother's body at the very beginning of a human life surely has ominous implications.

Now, what about the safety of 2,4,5-T itself? Admittedly, the dioxin contaminant seems to be a residue from one stage of its manufacture. But if by some future chemical miracle the very last trace of dioxin could be removed from the finished 2,4,5-T, would the resultant "pure" 2,4,5-T be harmless? The fact seems to be that even then 2,4,5-T, as produced in this country, would have to be viewed with suspicion, for the breakdown products of 2,4,5-T, when subjected to heat and other conditions, are themselves capable, according to a number of responsible biologists, of producing dioxin. Given this potential, the ultimate folly in our defoliation operations in Vietnam was possibly achieved during 1965 and 1966, when the military made large-scale efforts in two defoliated areas to create fire storms—that is, fires so huge that all the oxygen in those areas would be exhausted. The apparent intention was to render the soil barren. (A fire storm would also, of course, have the result of burning or suffocating any living beings remaining in the area.) Operation Sherwood Forest, conducted in 1965, was an attempt to burn a defoliated section of the Boi Loi Woods. In October, 1966, the military began Operation Pink Rose, a similar project. Neither of the projects, in which tons of napalm were thrown down on top of the residue of tons of sprayed 2,4,5-T, succeeded in creating the desired effect; whether they released into the atmosphere dioxin produced by the breakdown products of the 2,4,5-T will probably never be known.

There are also less spectacular ways in which conditions suitable for the release of dioxin in Vietnam may have been created. For example, after areas accessible by road have been defoliated, woodcutters move in to chop up the dead timber, which is then sold in nearby towns and villages as fuel in the form of charcoal or firewood. Large quantities of fuel derived from defoliated areas are said to have been entering Saigon for years. Since the fires are customarily tended by Vietnamese women, and since many of them are certainly pregnant, the hazards to health and to the lives of unborn children surely cannot be ignored.

In the United States, the potential hazards from the present use of 2,4,5-T are considerably less than they are in Vietnam. In the first place, the recommended concentrations of 2,4,5-T for spraying here are, as I have pointed out, about a thirteenth of what the Vietnamese population is sometimes subjected to. And, in the second place, a great deal, if not most, of the 2,4,5-T that would otherwise have been sprayed on American crops and grazing areas has for several years been sent to Vietnam. However, the shortage of 2,4,5-T in this country does not necessarily mean that the potential hazards are at a minimum. The substances known as the trichlorophenols and compounds of pentachlorophenol, which officials of the F.D.A. believe may be chemical precursors of dioxin under certain thermal and other conditions, are used widely in the manufacture of a large variety of consumer products, ranging from paper to laundry starch and hair shampoo. Dow Chemical puts out a whole line of polychlorophenolic chemicals known as Dowicide Products. Monsanto Chemical also puts out a line of pentachlorophenol substances, known as Penta Compounds. Since a very great many consumer products wind up being burned sooner or later, and since the polychlorophenolic compounds are suspected of being capable, under particular thermal and other conditions, of releasing dioxin, the alarming question arises whether, and to what extent, dioxin is being released into the environment through the atmosphere. Pentachlorophenol, used in certain herbicides, is readily decomposed in sunlight, and in its breakdown process a number of products, including chemical precursors of chlorodibenzo-p-dioxin compounds, are produced. Because of these factors, a whole range of pesticides, as well as of herbicides, now must come under suspicion of producing dioxin compounds.

Although the chemical companies that manufacture 2,4,5-T have long taken pride in pointing out that 2,4,5-T itself is quite readily decomposable in soil, the crucial matters of how stable the dioxin contaminant is and to what extent it is cumulative in animal tissue have apparently been neglected. Consequently, the fact that traces of compounds virtually indistinguishable from dioxin have already been detected in this country in the human food chain—in the livers of chickens and in edible oils—clearly indicates that dioxin should be considered a hazard to man. Why, under all these inauspicious circumstances, the production and the use here and in Vietnam of 2,4,5-T has not summarily been stopped by the United States government is hard to understand.

Sincerely,
THOMAS WHITESIDE

APPENDICES

Report of the Secretary's Commission on Pesticides and Their Relationship to Environmental Health

(U.S. Department of Health, Education, and Welfare, December 1969)

Teratogenicity of Pesticides

SUMMARY AND CONCLUSIONS

Teratology deals with the etiology and development of congenital malformations. Congenital malformations are generally defined as gross structural abnormalities of prenatal origin, present at birth or manifesting shortly after, which kill or disable. In a broader sense, teratogenesis is considered to include histological, biochemical, and functional abnormalities of prenatal origin.

Congenital malformations present obvious personal, medical, and social stresses. Additionally, it has been recently estimated that the costs to society of one severely malformed child, in terms of medical and other care and deprivation of potential earnings, amount to several hundred thousand dollars.

There are now well over 400 substances that, in various forms and combinations, are currently used as pesticides.

Pesticides may represent an important potential teratogenic hazard. Therefore any teratogenic pesticide to which the population is exposed should be promptly identified so that appropriate precautions can be taken to prevent risk of human exposure. It is feasible to test these substances for teratogenic effects in test animals so that potential hazards to human health can be evaluated.

For these and other reasons detailed in the report, we conclude that:

a. All currently used pesticides should be tested for teratogenicity in the near future in 2 or more mammalian species chosen on the basis of the closest metabolic and pharmacologic similarity to human beings possible. Pesticides should be tested at various concentrations including levels substantially higher than those to which the human population are likely to be exposed. Test procedures should also reflect routes related to human exposure. Apart from the obvious route of ingestion, attention should be directed to other routes of exposure, including inhalation exposures from pesticide aerosols and vaporizing pesticide strips used domestically and exposures from skin absorption. Parenteral administration is an appropriate test route for pesticides to which humans are exposed by inhalation, or for pesticides which are systemically absorbed following ingestion.

b. The use of currently registered pesticides to which humans are exposed and which are found to be teratogenic by suitable test procedures in one or more mammalian species should be immediately restricted to prevent risk of human exposure. Such pesticides, in current use, include Captan, Carbaryl; the butyl, isopropyl, and isooctyl esters of 2,4-D Folpet; mercurials; PCNB; and 2,4,5-T. The teratogenicity of 2,4-D, the other salts and esters of both 2,4-D and 2,4,5-T, and that of IPC should be investigated further.

c. Pesticides found to be inactive after appropriate testing can be considered as provisionally safe, unless other evidence of teratogenicity develops.

d. No new pesticide should be registered until tested for teratogenicity by suitable procedures. Any pesticide found to be teratogenic should only be used in circumstances where risk of human exposure is minimal.

e. Efforts should be made to improve and standardize procedures for teratogenicity testing and population monitoring.

A scientific group or commission should be charged with responsibility for continued surveillance of the whole problem of pesticide teratogenesis.

METHODOLOGIES FOR TERATOGENICITY TESTING

Introduction

Prior to 1963, the Food and Drug Administration did not require evaluation of teratogenicity. As a result of the thalidomide disaster, the need for data on teratogenicity became evident. In 1963, the President's Science Advisory Committee on "Use of Pesticides" recommended that toxicity studies on pesticides include effects on reproduction through at least 2 generations in at least 2 species of warm-blooded animals. Observations to be included were effects on fertility, size and weight of litters, fetal mortality, teratogenicity, and growth and development of sucklings and weanlings. Such toxicity studies including the three-generation procedure were not designed primarily to detect teratogenicity and thus may not be appropriate.

The potential teratogenicity of chemicals may be detected by two complementary approaches. First, chemicals or other agents may be administered to experimental animals to determine whether they induce prenatal damage. Secondly, and on a *post hoc* basis, human populations may be epidemiologically surveyed to detect geographical or temporal clusters of unusual types or frequencies of congenital malformations. Combinations of these approaches are likely to ensure early detection and identification of teratogenic hazards.

Experimentally, a complex of factors are needed to elicit

teratogenic effects. These relate to gestation period, geno-type of the pregnant animals, dosage, mode of administration and metabolic transformation of teratogen. For example, teratogens may be effective only at a certain dose range, whether high or low, narrow or wide, below which development is apparently undisturbed, and above which death *in utero* results.

Most agents are teratogenic only in the developmentally labile early period of gestation, during which active organogenesis occurs. In humans, this sensitive period extends approximately from the end of the first week of pregnancy to the 12th week. Other circumstances may also influence the effectiveness of human teratogens, such as maternal nutritional, demographic, socioeconomic, and cultural factors, physiological states, and temporal and seasonal situations. Thus a potential teratogen may manifest its effect only when particular conditions conjoin.

The relationship between human exposure to a teratogen and subsequent induction of congenital abnormalities is generally not obvious. Any one teratogen may produce a multiplicity of effects and any specific effect may be produced by various teratogens. In test animals, the teratogenic response may differ from species to species. In humans, differences in genetic, metabolic, and environmental influences may contribute to a variety of specific effects from exposure to a particular teratogenic agent. Induced and spontaneous effects may be difficult to distinguish. The teratogenicity of thalidomide might have been missed had it not produced malformations rarely encountered; additionally, only a fraction of the pregnant women who took thalidomide had defective children.

Consequently, further data on the possible teratogenic effects of pesticides in experimental animals are urgently needed to provide a basis for evaluating potential hazards to human health. . . .

Literature Review

Bionetics animal studies

Bionetics Research Laboratories of Litton Industries, during 1965–68 under a contract for the National Cancer Institute (NCI Contracts PH 43–64–57 and PH 43–67–735), tested various pesticides and related compounds for teratogenic effects. These studies were designed as large-scale screening tests. The Bionetics data were re-analyzed stasitically to account for litter effects. The results of this statistical re-evaluation are presented in this section. More detailed material on these pesticides will be published in the future.

a. Summary of findings from Bionetic animal studies. Tested more extensively than other pesticides, 2,4,5-T was clearly teratogenic as evidenced by production of statistically increased proportions of litters affected, and increased proportions of abnormal fetuses within litters in both DMSO and Honey for both C57BL/6 and AKR mice. In particular, cleft palate and cystic kidneys were significantly more prevalent. In addition, a hybrid strain resulting from a C57BL/6 female and AKR male showed significant increases in anomalies, in particular cystic kidney, when administered at 113 mg./kg. of body weight in DMSO.

Additionally, 2,4,5-T was tested in Sprague-Dawley rats. When given orally at dosages of 4.6, 10.0 and 46.4 mg./kg. on days 10 through 15 of gestation, an excessive fetal mortality, up to 60 percent at the highest dose, and high incidence of abnormalities in the survivors was obtained. The incidence of fetuses with kidney anomalies was three-fold that of the controls, even with the smallest dosage tested.

PCNB produced an increase in renal agenesis between litters, and within litters, when administered orally from days 6–14 or days 6–10 of pregnancy. However, renal agenesis was not produced when PCNB was administered only from days 10–14 of pregnancy. These effects were produced in only the C57BL/6 strain of mice.

Other pesticides producing a statistically significant increase in the proportion of litters containing abnormal fetuses and in the increased incidence of abnormal fetuses within litters were: Captan, Folpet, 2,4-D isooctyl ester, 2,4-D butyl ester, 2,4-D isopropyl ester, carbaryl (Sevin), and IPC. . . . The results for carbaryl and for IPC were less consistent than for other compounds. (The pesticides 2,4,5-T, PCNB, captan, Folpet, carbaryl, IPC, and the butyl and isopropyl esters of 2,4-D were statistically significant at the .01 level, for one or more tests. This criterion is similar to that adopted by the Technical Panel on Carcinogenesis, Chapter 5, to identify "positive" compounds. The isooctyl ester of 2,4-D was significant at the 0.05 level.)

Compounds inducing only an increase in the proportion of abnormal fetuses within litters were: a-naphthol, and 2,4-D methyl ester. The statistical significance of these results was relatively weak; further study is required before any conclusions can be reached. Similarly, 2,4-D produced only an increase in the proportion of abnormal litters during 1965 in AKR mice. Due to the teratogenic activity of certain of its esters, 2,4-D should be studied further.

Carbaryl plus piperonyl butoxide did not show an overall increase in nonspecific anomalies, but resulted in significantly more cystic kidneys for doses above 10 mg./kg. carbaryl plus 100 μl./kg. piperonyl butoxide.

It must be emphasized that failure to detect statistically significant increases of anomalies may be due to insensitivity resulting from experimental variation and small numbers of litters tested. In addition, higher fetal mortality among some of the "negative" compounds may be selectively eliminating abnormal fetuses.

b. Methods. Four strains of mice were used: C57BL/6, AKR, C3H, and A/Ha. Most of the studies were performed with the C57BL/6 strain. A hybrid fetus resulting from mating a C57BL/6 female with an AKR male was used to study a few compounds. More restricted studies were also made on Sprague-Dawley rats; results of these with reference to 2,4,5-T are considered separately.

Most compounds were administered subcutaneously in 0.1 ml. solutions of dimethylsulfoxide (DMSO). Water soluble compounds were administered in saline, and sometimes also in DMSO. Compounds administered orally were given by gavage in 0.1 ml. in a 50-percent honey solution. Groups of positive controls and untreated controls were included, as well as controls receiving only DMSO, saline, or honey. While controls were run periodically throughout the duration of the study, compounds and controls were not matched with respect to either route or date of administration.

Virgin females were used in these studies. The onset of pregnancy was determined by detection of vaginal plugs. Compounds were administered daily from the sixth to the 14th day of pregnancy (15th day for AKR mice). Mice were sacrificed on the 18th day (19th day for AKR mice) of gestation. On sacrifice, fetuses were examined for anomalies. Approximately two-thirds of the fetuses were then stored in Bouin's solution until necropsy. Remaining fetuses were stained with alizarin red S after proper processing. Numbers of resorption sites and dead fetuses were also scored.

c. Statistical analysis. All analyses were performed on a *per* litter basis rather than a *per* fetus basis, since initial investigation indicated that the occurrences of anomalies among fetuses within litters were correlated. The large litter-to-litter variation may reflect some maternal effect, an indication of the effective dose level of the compound actually reaching the fetuses, experimental variation, or, as is most likely, some combination of the three factors.

While there were no statistically significant time trends within the various control groups in terms of the onset of fetal anomalies in the C57BL/6 mice, the incidence of fetal mortality was certainly time-dependent in this strain, with 1965 being characterized by a low incidence of prenatal deaths. Furthermore, there was a period of approximately 6 months, extending from the latter part of 1965 into early 1966, during which no control animals were tested. During this period a change in the substrain of

C57BL/6 mice used in the study took place. Finally, among abnormal litters, as defined by litters containing at least one abnormal fetus, there was some suggestion that the distribution of abnormal fetuses *per* litter was stochastically larger in the DMSO controls than it was in the untreated controls. Thus, the possibility exists of a time/strain/solvent interaction that is undetectable in the controls because the level of background teratologic activity is relatively low. This potential interaction effect could either enhance or dissipate the effect of any given compound, depending on the conditions under which it was administered. Thus, the data were necessarily separated by both time period and solvent for the purposes of analysis. Similarly, an increase in fetal anomalies in the DMSO controls of the AKR mice was noted after November 1966. Thus, the AKR data were analyzed separately in two time periods.

It should be noted that not all compounds were administered on more than one occasion or in more than one solvent or strain. Thus, in general the compounds in the study cannot be compared for teratogenic potential, since those that were tested extensively were more likely to show some adverse effect and, perhaps, less likely to appear consistent over time, solvent, and/or strain.

As noted, approximately two-thirds of the fetuses were stored in Bouin's solution until necropsied; the remainder being stained with alizarin red. However, in many instances the proportion of necropsied fetuses was slightly higher for the compound under investigation than for the corresponding controls. It is doubtful if this discrepancy could have any appreciable effect on the conclusions since the incidence of anomalies detectable only by necropsy among control animals was relatively low. Furthermore, if all of the control and test mice had been necropsied, the significance of the differences observed in this study would be intensified. Thus, no effort was made to correct for inequalities in the necropsy/stain ratio in the present analysis. Additionally, no attempt was made to correct for differences in litter sizes or sex-ratios within litters, since both of these factors may, at least in part, reflect effects of the compound under test.

d. Results. Data for pesticides yielding a statistically increased level of anomalies in C57BL/6 and AKR mice are listed in tables 1 and 2, respectively. The proportion of abnormal litters gives the proportion of litters containing one or more abnormal fetuses, as a measure of the prevalence of anomalies across litters. The proportion of abnormal fetuses *per* litter gives a measure of the prevalence of anomalies within litters. The proportion of abnormal fetuses *per* litter for litters containing abnormal fetuses gives a measure of the prevalence of anomalies within affected litters. A significant increase of dead fetuses and resorptions is also listed. Some tests were conducted on only one particular day or on adjacent days as listed. Eye anomalies, mainly microphthalmia and anophthalmia, accounted for approximately 50 percent of the individual anomalies in C57BL/6 mice. To a large extent, results in table 1 reflect changes in the incidence of eye anomalies. Yet, when the data were analyzed excluding fetuses with microphthalmia only, there were no striking changes in the results. In the last column of table 1, statistically significant increase in various types of anomalies other than eye anomalies are listed. The positive controls, trypan blue and ethyleneimine, table 1, and 6-aminonicotinamide, table 2, showed elevated levels of anomalies, although the latter control did not yield consistent results over all dose levels.

Only those test conditions which resulted in statistically elevated incidences of anomalies are listed in tables 1 and 2. Some compounds gave no increase in anomalies (based on the overall incidence if tested in both time periods) when tested in other solvents, strains, or dose levels (table 3). It must be emphasized that failure to detect a statistically significant increase in anomalies may only be a reflection of experimental insensitivity due to experimental and biological variation and insufficient number of litters. Thus, compounds showing no increases cannot be considered nonteratogenic. For example, trypan blue in DMSO at the highest dose level tested, 37.5 mg./kg., did not show

TABLE 1.—*Tests which displayed significant increases of anomalies (C57BL/6 mice)*

Compound	Solvent	Dose per kg of body weight	Proportion of abnormal litters			Proportion of abnormal fetuses per litter			Proportion of abnormal fetuses per litter in abnormal litters			Increased mortality	Tests repeated over time	No. of live litters		Increased anomalies other than eye
			1965	1966–68	Total	1965	1966–68	Total	1965	1966–68	Total			1965	1966–68	
Negative controls:																
Untreated	None		.42	.39	.40	.08	.11	.10	.18	.28	.25			26	69	
Controls	DMSO		.53	.41	.46	.16	.12	.13	.33	.28	.29			70	112	
Do.	Saline		.52	.37	.43	.13	.10	.11	.24	.28	.26			31	46	
Do.	Honey			.47	.47	.15	.15	.15	.32	.32	.32				32	
Positive controls:																
Trypan blue	DMSO	5.0 mg	.60		.60	.32		.32	.54		.54	Yes		5		Hydrocephaly.
Do.	DMSO	12.5 mg	.86		.86	.44***		.44***	.52**		.52**	Yes		7		Hydrocephaly.
Do.	DMSO	37.5 mg	.60		.60	.36		.36	.60		.60	Yes		5		
Do.	Saline	5.0 mg	1.00		1.00	.61***		.61***	.61**		.61**			5		
Do.	do.	12.5 mg	.71		.71	.49***		.49***	.69***		.69***	Yes		7		Hydrocephaly.
Do.	do.	37.5 mg	.71		.71	.33*		.33*	.40**		.40**	Yes		7		Hydrocephaly.
Ethyleneimine	do.	4.64 µl	1.00*		1.00*	.49***		.49***	.49***		.49***	Yes	No	7		
Experimental:																
2,4,5-T	DMSO	113 mg		.79**	.79**		.50***	.50***		.71***	.71***	Yes	No		14	Cleft palate cystic kidney.
2,4,5-T	Honey	46.4 mg		1.00*	1.00*		.37**	.37**		.37***	.37***		No		6	Cleft palate cystic kidney.
2,4,5-T	do.	113 mg		1.00**	1.00**		.70***	.70***		.70***	.70***	Yes			9	Cleft palate cystic kidney.
PCNB (days 6–14)	do.	215 mg		.88*	.88*		.25*	.25*		.29	.29		No		8	Renal agenesis.
PCNB (days 6–14)	do.	464 mg		.67**	.67**		.25***	.25***		.38	.38		No		12	Renal agenesis.
PCNB (days 6–10)	do.	464 mg		1.00***	1.00***		.38***	.38***		.37	.37		No		10	
Captan	DMSO	100 mg	.61	.77**	.71***	.58**	.27	.35***	.58**	.44	.49**	Yes		6	18	
Folpet	DMSO	100 mg	1.00*		1.00*	.24		.24	.24		.24			6	13	
2,4-D Isooctyl ester	DMSO	48 µl	1.00*		1.00*	.24		.24	.24		.24			6		
2,4-D Isooctyl ester	DMSO	130 µl		.75**	.75**		.28**	.28***		.41*	.41*				15	
2,4-D Butyl ester	DMSO	100 µl		.75**	.75**		.25**	.25***		.34	.34				20	
2,4-D Isopropyl ester	DMSO	94 µl		.70**	.70**		.26**	.26***		.37*	.37*				20	Agnathia.

Compound	Solvent / Dose per kg of body weight	Prop. of abnormal litters †11/66	12/66††	Total	Prop. of abnormal fetuses per litter †11/66	12/66††	Total	Prop. of abnormal fetuses per litter in abnormal litters †11/66	12/66††	Total	Increased mortality over time	Tests repeated over time	No. of live litters †11/66	12/66††	Special anomalies
Carbaryl	DMSO..100 mg	1.00*	.54	.71**	.46***	.16	.26**	.46*	.29	.37			6	11	Hydrocephaly, skeletal
IPC	DMSO..850 mg	1.00**	.43	.71**	.46***	.09	.27**	.46*		.46*			7	7	
α-Naphthol	DMSO..10 mg	.88		.86	.83*		.39*	.88		.38			7	7	
2,4-D Methyl ester	DMSO..106 mg		.83	.83		.30*	.30*		.36	.36	No		7	6	
Carbaryl + Piperonyl Butoxide	DMSO..10 µg +		.50	.60		.13	.13		.26	.26	No			6	} Cystic kidney
Do	DMSO..46.4 mg + 464 µl		.50	.50		.10	.10		.21	.21				12	

Significance level: *(.10). **(.05). ***(.01).

TABLE 2.—Tests which displayed significant increases of anomalies (AKR mice)

Compound	Solvent / Dose per kg of body weight	Prop. of abnormal litters †11/66	12/66††	Total	Prop. of abnormal fetuses per litter †11/66	12/66††	Total	Prop. of abnormal fetuses per litter in abnormal litters †11/66	12/66††	Total	Increased mortality over time	Tests repeated over time	No. of live litters †11/66	12/66††	Special anomalies
Negative controls:															
Control	DMSO	.05	.37	.21	.01	.06	.03	.11	.16	.15			37	35	
Do	Honey		.00	.00		.00	.00							12	
Positive controls:															
6-amino-nicotina-mide	DMSO..34 mg	.50***		.50***	.31**		.31**	.55		.55			9		Cleft palate.
6-amino-nicotina-mide (1)	DMSO..68 mg	.00		.00	.00		.00						7		
Experimental:															
2,4,5-T	DMSO..113 mg	.50***	1.00**	.71***	.20**	.40**	.29***	.40*	.40**	.40*			8	6	Cleft palate
2,4,5-T	Honey..113 mg	1.00***	1.00**	1.00***	.54***	.54**	.54***	.40**	.54	.54		yes		6	Cleft palate
2,4-D	DMSO..98 mg	.43**	.29	.36*	.12	.05	.08	.28	.16	.23			7	7	

*Significance Level .10. **Significance Level .05. ***Significance Level .01. †Through 11/66. ††After 11/66
Note: (1) With the .68 mg/kg dose, as compared to the .34 mg/kg dose, fewer implantations and a higher fetal mortality were encountered, resulting in fewer live fetuses per litter.

an increase in anomalies, possibly due to higher fetal mortality. Standard corrected 2 × 2 chi-square tests were used to compare the proportion of abnormal litters for the compound with the controls in the same solvent. In the cases where tests were conducted in two time periods, the results from the two chi-squares were combined. The levels of statistical significance for the combined tests are listed under the total column for proportion of abnormal litters.

The distribution of the proportion of abnormal fetuses per litter (tables 1 and 2) for compounds were compared with the appropriate control distribution by use of the nonparametric Mann-Whitney U-test. This test requires that the proportion of abnormal fetuses per litter is independent from litter to litter, but requires no assumption about the frequency distribution of these proportions. Again, where litters were run in both time periods, the significance level for the combined tests is given under the total column. Bracketed data include groups which were combined before statistical tests were conducted.

Excerpts from the Bionetics Laboratories Report

From Volume III
Evaluation of the Teratogenic Activity of Selected Pesticides and Industrial Chemicals in Mice & Rats

2,4,5-T—BRL No. 061

(TABLE A-22 ORIGINAL BIONETICS REPORT)

This compound was given by the oral route to BL6 mice at dosages of 46.4 and 113 mg/kg and to AKR mice at 113 mg/kg. It was given by subcutaneous injection to BL6 mice at dosages of 21.5 and 113 mg/kg and to AKR mice and B6AK hybrids at 113 mg/kg. It was also given subcutaneously to C3H mice at 215 mg/kg, but there were too few of these to merit inclusion in the discussion which follows. Administration was for eight days (6th through 14th) in most cases; for nine days (6th through 15th) in some; and for five days (10th through 14th) in one case—the details are indicated in the tabulated results. Subcutaneous administration used DMSO as a vehicle; oral used 50% honey.

With the single exception of the lowest dosage used (21.5 mg/kg to BL6 subcutaneously) all dosages, routes, and strains resulted in increased incidence of abnormal fetuses. The incidence of cleft palate was high at the 113 mg/kg dosage, but not at lower levels. The incidence of cystic kidney was also high except in the AKR strain and in the BL6 mice which received 46.4 mg/kg orally. Fetal mortality was increased in all groups given 113 mg/kg for eight or nine days, but not in mice (BL6) given this dosage for only five days nor in the two groups of BL6 mice given lesser dosages (46.4 mg/kg orally and 21.5 mg/kg subcutaneously).

Most fetal and maternal measurements showed inconsistent changes from which no conclusions can be drawn. In contrast there was a highly consistent decrease in maternal weight gain in BL6 mice given 113 mg/kg by either route. Lower dosages and the AKR strain showed either no change or a slight increase. All dosages, strains, and routes showed an increase in the maternal liver weight and this led to a further study discussed separately below.

These results imply a hazard of teratogenesis in the use of this compound. The problems of extrapolation preclude definition of the hazard on the basis of these studies, but its existence seems clear.

LIVER WEIGHT STUDY (TABLE A-22)

The observed influence of 2,4,5-T on maternal liver weight as mentioned above raised a question as to its effect on the fetal liver. This was answered by a study carried out in BL6 mice using subcutaneous injections of DMSO solutions at a dosage of 113 mg/kg only. The period of administration was lengthened to cover the period from the 9th through 17th day of gestation. Separate control groups were used concurrently. Except for the inclusion of fetal liver weight, measurements were made as previously described.

The fetal livers of the 2,4,5-T treated mice weighed significantly more than those of controls given DMSO only and the weights of the whole fetuses were significantly less. Correspondingly, there was an increase in the fetal liver weight expressed as percent of body weight.

Other observations were consistent with those reported above. The incidence of abnormal fetuses was unusually high as were those of cleft palate and cystic kidney.

RATS—SPRAGUE-DAWLEY STRAIN (TABLE A-22)

Because of the potential importance of the findings in mice, an additional study was carried out in rats of the Sprague-Dawley strain. Using dosages of 21.5 and 46.4 mg/kg suspended in 50% honey and given by the oral route on the 6th through 15th days of gestation, we observed excessive fetal mortality (almost 80%) and a high incidence of abnormalities in the survivors. When the beginning of administration was delayed until the 10th day, fetal mortality was somewhat less, but still quite high even when dosage was reduced to 4.6 mg/kg. The incidence of abnormal fetuses was threefold that in controls even with the smallest dosage and shortest period used. Fetal and maternal measurements showed only occasional instances of significant differences from controls except in the case of maternal liver weight which was consistently increased in all 2,4,5-T treated animals.

It seems inescapable that 2,4,5-T is teratogenic in this strain of rats when given orally at the dosage schedules used here. These findings lend emphasis to the hazard implied by the results of studies on mice.

Rat Study of the Sprague-Dawley Strain

COMPOUND	NON-TREATED	HONEY	HONEY	2,4,5-T	2,4,5-T	2,4,5-T	2,4,5-T	2,4,5-T	2,4,5-T
Strain Sprague-Dawley	..	..	..	..	..	..	..	..	..
Dosage mg/kg	..	200†	200†	4.6	10.0	21.5	21.5	46.4	46.4
Vehicle/Route	..	Honey/po	Honey/po	Honey/po	Honey/po	Honey/po	Honey/po	Honey/po	Honey
Administration Days Gestation	..	10–15	6–15	10–15	10–15	10–15	6–15	10–15	6–15
No. Litters	7	14	6	8	7	3	4	6	2
Total No. Fetuses	60	122	46	66	50	20	12	16	4
Percent abnormal fetuses									
Total	10	13	7	39	78	90	92	100	75
P....	—	0.5	0.9	0.001	0.001	0.001	—	—	—
With renal anomalies...	10	13	6	36	46	55	42	50	25
Anomalies									
No. observed									
Renal									
Enlarged pelvis.........	7	16	3	16	9	4	5	5	0
Cystic kidney...........	0	1	0	11	15	7	0	3	1
Cleft palate...............	0	0	0	0	0	0	0	0	1
Hemorrhagic GI tract.......	0	0	0	3	27	18	10	15	2

†μl/rat

Employment of Riot Control Agents, Flame, Smoke, Antiplant Agents, and Personnel Detectors in Counterguerrilla Operations

Department of the Army Training Circular TC 3-16 April 1969

Antiplant Agent Operations

51. General. Antiplant agents are chemical agents which possess a high offensive potential for destroying or seriously limiting the production of food and defoliating vegetation. These compounds include herbicides that kill or inhibit the growth of plants; plant growth regulators that either regulate or inhibit plant growth, sometimes causing plant death; desiccants that dry up plant foliage; and soil sterilants that prevent or inhibit the growth of vegetation by action with the soil. Military applications for antiplant agents are based on denying the enemy food and concealment.

52. Antiplant Agents in Use.

a. ORANGE.

(1) *Description.* Agent ORANGE is the Standard A agent. It is composed of a 50:50 mixture of the n-butyl esters of 2,4-D and 2,4,5-T (app D and C1, TM 3-215).

ORANGE appears as a dark-brown oily liquid which is insoluble in water but miscible in oils such as diesel fuel. It weighs about 10.75 pounds per gallon and becomes quite viscous as the temperature drops, solidifying at 45° F. It is noncorrosive, of low volatility, and nonexplosive, but deteriorates rubber.

(2) *Rate of application.* The recommended rate of application of ORANGE is 3 gallons per acre. This may vary depending on the type of vegetation (app C). In some situations better coverage may be obtained by diluting ORANGE with diesel fuel oil, which results in a less viscous solution that is dispersed in smaller droplets. Dilution may also be required when using dispersion equipment which does not permit the flow rate to be conveniently adjusted to 3 gallons per acre. See discussion of application methods in paragraphs 57 and 58.

(3) *Effect on foliage.* ORANGE penetrates the waxy covering of leaves and is absorbed into the plant system. It affects the growing points of the plant, resulting in its death. Rains occurring within the first hour after spraying will not reduce the effectiveness of ORANGE to the extent that they reduce the effectiveness of aqueous solutions. Broadleaf plants are highly susceptible to ORANGE. Some grasses can be controlled but require a much higher dose rate than broadleaf plants. Susceptible plants exhibit varying degrees of susceptibility to ORANGE. Death of a given plant may occur within a week or less, or may require up to several months depending on the plant's age, stage of growth, susceptibility, and the dose rate. See employment considerations in paragraphs 53 through 55.

(4) *Safety precautions and decontamination.* ORANGE is relatively nontoxic to man or animals. No injuries have been reported to personnel exposed to aircraft spray. Personnel subject to splashes from handling the agent need not be alarmed, but should shower and change clothes at a convenient opportunity. ORANGE is noncorrosive to metals but will remove aircraft paint and walkway coatings. Contaminated aircraft should be washed with soapy water to remove the agent. Rubber hoses and other rubber parts

of transfer and dissemination equipment will deteriorate and require replacement, since ORANGE softens rubber.

b. *BLUE (Phytar 560G)*.

(1) *Description*. Agent BLUE is an aqueous solution containing about 3 pounds per gallon of the sodium salt of cacodylic acid, the proper amount of surfactant (a substance which increases the effectiveness of the solution), and a neutralizer to prevent corrosion of metal spray apparatus. BLUE is the agent normally used for crop destruction.

(2) *Rate of application*. BLUE may be sprayed as received from the manufacturer without dilution, if desired. The recommended application rate for crop destruction is about 1 to 2 gallons per acre (app C). However, much higher use rates of BLUE are required to kill tall grasses, such as elephant grass or sugarcane, because of the large masses of vegetation. For hand-spray operations, two gallons of BLUE diluted with water to make 50 gallons will give a solution that can be dispersed by hand at a rate equivalent to approximately 1 to 3 gallons of pure agent per acre.

(3) *Effect on foliage*. Enough BLUE applied to any kind of foliage will cause it to dry and shrivel, but the agent is more effective against grassy plants than broadleaf varieties. Best results are obtained when the plant is thoroughly covered, since the agent kills by absorption of moisture from the leaves. The plants will die within 2 to 4 days or less and can then be burned if permitted to dry sufficiently. BLUE in low dose rates can also prevent grain formation in rice without any apparent external effect. The plant develops normally but does not yield a crop. Spray rates higher than about one-half gallon per acre usually kill the crop. Although BLUE can produce relatively rapid defoliation, regrowth may occur again in about 30 days. Repeated spraying is necessary to provide a high degree of continuous plant kill.

(4) *Safety precautions and decontamination*. Normal sanitary precautions should be followed when handling BLUE. Although it contains a form of arsenic, BLUE is

relatively nontoxic. It should not be taken internally, however. Any material that gets on the hands, face, or other parts of the body should be washed off at the first opportunity. Clothes that become wet with a solution of BLUE should be changed. Aircraft used for spraying this solution should be washed well afterward. When WHITE is added to BLUE, a precipitate forms that will clog the system. If the same spray apparatus is to be used for spraying agents WHITE and BLUE, the system must be flushed to assure that all residue of the previous agent is removed.

c. WHITE (Tordon 101).

(1) *Description.* The active ingredients of agent WHITE are 20 percent picloram and 80 percent isopropylamine salt of 2, 4-D. Active ingredients constitute about 25 percent of the solution. A surfactant is also present. WHITE is soluble in water, noncorrosive, nonflammable, nonvolatile, immiscible in oils, and more viscous than ORANGE at the same temperature.

(2) *Rate of application.* WHITE usually should be applied at a rate of 3 to 5 gallons per acre on broadleaf vegetation. However, the rate may vary depending on the type of flora. Quantities required to control jungle vegetation may vary from 5 to 12 gallons per acre. This quantity exceeds the spray capability of most aircraft spray systems for a single pass. It is usually unfeasible in large-scale military operations to apply such large volumes. For ground-based spray operations, however, high volumes are necessary. Hand-spray operations cannot evenly cover a whole acre with only 3 gallons of solution. Three gallons of WHITE diluted to a 30-gallon solution can be more easily sprayed over an area of one acre. The manufacturer recommends diluting WHITE with sufficient water to make a 10-gallon solution for each gallon of agent.

(3) *Effect on foliage.* WHITE kills foliage in the same manner as ORANGE, since 80 percent of the active ingredient is 2,4-D. PICLORAM is more effective than 2,4-D, but acts slower. WHITE is effective on many plant species, and equal to or more effective than ORANGE on the more woody species. The material must be absorbed

through the leaves. The water solution does not penetrate the waxy covering of leaves as well as oily mixtures and is more easily washed off by rain.

(4) *Safety precautions and decontamination.* WHITE exhibits a low hazard from accidental ingestion. However, it may cause some irritation if splashed into the eyes. Should eye contact occur, flush with plenty of water. Splashes on the skin should be thoroughly washed with soap and water at the first opportunity. Contaminated clothing should be washed before reuse. When WHITE is used in the same equipment as BLUE, all of the WHITE should be removed before using BLUE. The two agents produce a white precipitate that will clog spray systems.

d. *Soil Sterilants.*

(1) *BROMACIL.*

(a) *Description.* BROMACIL is an odorless, noncorrosive, white crystalline solid, slightly soluble in water or diesel fuel oil. Three different forms are produced: HYVAR-X, a wettable powder containing 80-percent active ingredient; HYVAR-X-WS, a 50-percent active ingredient water-soluble powder; and UROX 'B', a liquid containing 4 pounds of active ingredient per gallon (app D).

(b) *Rate of application.* HYVAR-X is applied at a rate of 15 to 30 pounds per acre; HYVAR-X-WS, 24 to 48 pounds per acre; and UROX 'B', 3 to 6 gallons per acre. Spray concentrations of the agent as high as 50 to 150 pounds per 100 gallons of water or oil can be handled by aircraft-mounted spray systems. The 80-percent wettable powder is well suited for ground applications by power-driven decontaminating apparatus or turbine blower because it requires agitation while spraying to achieve the best results.

(2) *UROX 22.*

(a) *Description.* UROX 22 is a granular substance containing 22 percent monuron trichloroacetate.

(b) *Rate of application.* The manufacturer suggests using 150 to 200 pounds per acre.

(3) *Effect on foliage.* Soil sterilants act by absorption through the root system and therefore are most effective

under conditions of good soil moisture. They are relatively stable once absorbed into the soil. Soil sterilants kill vegetation and may prevent regrowth for periods of a few months to a year, depending on the quantity and soil conditions. They are most effective on grasses, but will control woody plants at higher application rates. Mechanical clearing by brush cutters or bulldozers is not necessary, but will help in getting the agent into the soil.

(4) *Safety precautions and handling.* Soil sterilants are only slightly corrosive to metals, but dispersion equipment should be thoroughly flushed after use. They are relatively nontoxic to humans, but respirator masks should be worn to prevent inhalation of dust during handling.

SECTION II

CONCEPTS OF EMPLOYMENT

53. General. *a.* The employment of antiplant agents must be carefully controlled by technically qualified personnel to avoid many undesirable aftereffects. FM 3-10 discusses the employment concepts, analysis of operations, and limitations of antiplant agents

b. Guerrilla operations rely heavily on locally produced crops for their food supply. Crop destruction can reduce the food supply and seriously affect the guerrilla's survival. Naturally dense vegetation in jungle areas is ideal for elusive hit-and-run tactics of the guerrilla. Removal or reduction of this concealment limits the guerrilla's capability to operate in the defoliated area

54. Employment Considerations. In addition to the concepts discussed in FM 3-10, the following points should be considered when planning the use of antiplant agents.

a. Type of Foliage. ORANGE is a wide-range, general-purpose agent which is effective on the many types of foliage found in jungle areas. WHITE is also considered a general-purpose herbicide, but it is generally slower than ORANGE. BLUE is most effective on the narrow leaf species: the grasses, sugarcane, rice, and other cereal grains.

b. When to Apply The best time to apply antiplant

agents is during the most active growing season. This corresponds roughly to the period from the appearance of new buds until 3 or 4 weeks before onset of the dry season. While spraying during the dry season does produce defoliation, vegetation is not killed as quickly as it is during the most active growing season. An exception would be in certain tropical lowland areas where water is plentiful and continuous growth exists; thus antiplant agents are effective throughout the year.

c. Effect on Nearby Crops. If the application of antiplant agents is on target to begin with, the main danger to nearby susceptible crops will be from drift. The main factors affecting agent drift are wind direction and speed, dissemination method (para 56 through 58), temperature gradient (TM 3-240), and the agent used. Conditions for dissemination of antiplant agents are usually most favorable during early morning hours (before 0800) while inversion temperature gradient prevails and the wind speed is still low (does not exceed 8 knots). A volatile antiplant agent may also produce drift effect even after the spray has settled on target. For example, the slight vaporization of ORANGE may produce drift damage, especially if nearby crops, such as rubber trees, cotton, melons, bananas, and other garden species, are *highly* susceptible to damage. Water-soluble agents BLUE and WHITE are not subject to vaporization after settling on target. Thus they can be more safely used near susceptible crops provided cautions such as wind direction are heeded, and a dissemination method that tends to produce the least amount of drift is used. Although soil sterilants do not drift, they should not be used closer than 100 meters to crops or cropland in a friendly area onto which drainage from treated areas flows.

d. Duration of Effect. Neither ORANGE, BLUE, nor WHITE can be considered "permanent" type antiplant agents. They act by direct contact with the plant. Defoliation resulting from aerial application of BLUE may be effective only until new growth appears. Defoliation resulting from aerial application of ORANGE or WHITE will usually be effective for one growing season, but may be effective for periods of approximately 9 months to 1 year. Soil sterilants, on the other hand, may be effective for periods of up to a year or more, because they are designed to be slowly dissolved by rainfall and remain active in the soil.

55. **Symptoms of Plant Injury.** The following symptoms of plant injury may be used to aid in evaluating the effectiveness of defoliation projects. Plants usually react to antiplant agents in one or more of these ways:

a. In some plants, leaves and growing stems form loops and coils or develop marked curvature.

b. Growing stems may remain green, but may swell, develop cracks, and form callous tissue.

c. Watery, translucent buds often appear at the crowns of some plants.

d. Spongy, enlarged roots may appear, turn black or gray, and rot.

e. Dead areas will form on the leaves wherever the spray droplets have settled on the leaf surface. A yellow ring may appear around the dead area, and gradually the entire leaf will develop yellow, brown, or red autumnal coloration and fall.

SECTION III

DISSEMINATION METHODS

56. **General.** Antiplant agents may be disseminated by various methods depending on the size of the area to be defoliated and whether the agent is in liquid, slurry, or solid form.

57. **Ground-Based Application.** Ground-based spray or dispersion methods are suited to small-scale operations such as defoliation around base camps or installations or clearing along routes of communication. These methods depend on easy access to the area on foot or by spray vehicle.

a. Hand broadcasting is the simplest way to disperse dry agents, such as soil sterilants, but is a rather time-consuming method.

b. A 3-gallon hand-pump sprayer is easy to use in areas

accessible by foot but where vehicles cannot enter. It is a slow method, however, and areas out of arm's reach are still inaccessible.

c. The M106 Mity Mite (para 26) may be used to disperse liquid or dry antiplant agents. Foot access to the area is required, but inaccessible areas may be covered to some extent, since the Mity Mite will spray a distance of about 50 feet.

d. A power-driven decontaminating apparatus (PDDA) may be used when the area is accessible to wheeled vehicles. It is especially suited for spraying soil sterilant in slurry form. The PDDA may also be used to spray liquid antiplant agents. WHITE and BLUE present no corrosion problems, but the apparatus must be well cleaned when changing between the two agents. ORANGE will soften the rubber parts, such as hoses and valve diaphragms, requiring their replacement after a while. Spraying ORANGE by PDDA also produces a fire hazard.

e. Commercial orchard sprayers, if available, may be used for spraying liquid solutions where ground access to vehicles is possible.

58. Aerial Spray Methods. Aerial spray methods are suited for large-scale operations since a larger area can be covered and ground access is not necessary. Aerial application methods are much more subject to weather conditions, such as wind direction and speed and temperature gradient, than are ground-based methods. Therefore, particular attention must be paid to the possibility of agent drift onto any nearby friendly crops. The height of attack, airspeed, and area coverage depend on weather and terrain conditions and pilot experience.

a. UC-123 Aircraft. UC-123B cargo aircraft fitted with internal tanks and external spray booms are used for large-scale defoliation and crop destruction operations. Using the present systems at an altitude of 150 feet and airspeed of 130 knots results in a spray rate of 3 gallons per acre.

b. FIDAL (Fixed-wing Insecticide Dispersal Apparatus, Liquid). The FIDAL is a Navy developed and tested system. It has not been standardized by the Army. When available, it can be used to supplement the spray capability of the C-123 systems. The FIDAL is hung on the AIE or A1H aircraft without modification. Each tank holds about 275 gallons and has its own ram air turbine to provide power for pumping the spray through a spray boom. Cost is much less than that of C-123 inboard systems, and spray missions do not tie up the aircraft since the tanks can be hung or removed in minutes.

c. Helicopter-Mounted Spray Systems.

(1) *HIDAL (Helicopter Insecticide Dispersal Apparatus, Liquid).* The HIDAL system is a 196-gallon spray system suitable for use in a UH-1 series helicopter. Helicopters are useful in spraying areas around installations that are not accessible to wheeled vehicles: minefields, barbed wire barriers, etc. The HIDAL is self-contained, has an adjustable spray rate, and can be installed and removed in a matter of minutes. It is a Navy developed system and has not been standardized by the Army.

(2) *AGAVENCO sprayer.* The AGAVENCO system has capabilities similar to those of the HIDAL and is presently being procured in a limited quantity. It has not been standardized.

d. Field Expedient Spray Systems. When systems such as the HIDAL are unavailable, field expedient spray systems that will perform adequately might be constructed.

(1) *UH-1 series aircraft.*

(a) A simple expedient spray system for a UH-1 type aircraft might consist of a 55-gallon drum (fig 41 and 42) fitted with a rubber hose which delivers the solution to a spray bar temporarily mounted across the skids. Slight pressurization of the drum will usually help empty the drum at a steady rate. A portable flamethrower pressure bottle or an AN-M4 compressor can be used for pressurizing, but a gage should be in the system to warn of excess pressure (no more than 8 to 12 psi should be used). The size and number of holes in the spray bar may be determined by trial and error; however, ⅛-inch holes spaced 6 inches apart will provide good results.

(b) Another field expedient system uses the tank and

16-foot boom of the HIDAL. A 25-gpm personnel carrier bilge pump delivers the agent, allowing 30 to 40 meters coverage in width.

2) *CH-47 aircraft.* An expedient spray system for a CH-47 aircraft might consist of a 500-gallon collapsible fuel bladder or a 400-gallon metal, skid-mounted tank. A power driven fuel transfer pump (50 to 100 gpm) can be used to deliver the antiplant agent to a spray bar attached to the ramp at the rear of the aircraft.

ANTIPLANT AGENT USE RATES[1]

Vegetation type	ORANGE	WHITE	BLUE[2]
Mangrove	1½ gal/acre	3-5 gal/acre	2 gal/acre
Highland trees (jungle)	3 gal/acre	3-5 gal/acre	2 gal/acre
Mixed mangrove, low land swamp, scrub trees.	3 gal/acre	3-5 gal/acre	2 gal/acre
Broadleaf crops (bean, manioc, corn, banana, tomato).	1 gal/acre	3-5 gal/acre	2 gal/acre
Rice	5 gal/acre	3-5 gal/acre	1 gal/acre
Mixed vegetables and rice.	3 gal/acre	3-5 gal/acre	2 gal/acre

[1] As recommended by the manufacturer.
[2] Usually applied in the field by C123 aircraft systems having fixed flow of 3 gal/acre.

COMPOSITION OF MILITARILY SIGNIFICANT ANTIPLANT AGENTS

Antiplant agent	Composition
ORANGE	50% 2,4-D (n-butyl-2,4-dichlorophenoxyacetate) 50% 2,4,5-T (n-butyl-2,4,5-trichlorophenoxyacetate).
WHITE	20% picloram (4-amino-3,5,6-trichloropicolinic acid) 80% 2.4-D (triisopropanolamine).
BLUE (Phytar 560G).	3 pounds per gallon of water of: 65% cacodylic acid (dimethylarsenic acid) 35% inert ingredients: sodium chloride, sodium and calcium sulfates, water.
BROMACIL ...	Active ingredient: 5-bromo-3-sec-butyl-6-methyluracil. HYVAR-X: 80% active ingredient. HYVAR-X-WS: 50% active ingredient. UROX 'B'—liquid, 4 pounds per gallon active ingredient
UROX 22......	22% monuron trichloroacetate, 78% inert ingredients.

Area Treated with Herbicides in South Vietnam 1962–1969

YEAR	DEFOLIATION	CROP DESTRUCTION
1962	4,940 *acres*	741 *acres*
1963	24,700	247
1964	83,486	10,374
1965	155,610	65,949
1966	741,247	101,517
1967	1,486,446	221,312
1968	1,267,110	63,726
1969 *(Jan.-Mar.)*	356,421	4,693
	4,119,960	468,559

Source: Military Assistance Command Vietnam Reports

Statement by Rear Admiral William E. Lemos
Policy Plans and National Security Council Affairs Office, Assistant Secretary (International Security Affairs) Department of Defense

---

Delivered before the Subcommittee on National Security Policy and Scientific Developments
Committee on Foreign Affairs
House of Representatives
First Session, 91st Congress
on Herbicide Operations

Turning now to the use of herbicides in Vietnam, one of the most difficult problems of military operations in South Vietnam is the inability to observe the enemy in the dense forest and jungle. Defoliating herbicides introduced in 1962 are capable of producing a significant improvement in vertical and horizontal visibility in the type of jungle found in South Vietnam. As viewed by an aerial observer, it is often impossible to see through the canopy to detect VC or NVA operations. In 6 to 8 weeks, after spraying with a herbicide, the observer will have good observation through the canopy. For ground observation, defoliation is highly effective in improving horizontal visibility.

The Herbicide Program in terms of effects produced has required an unusually small investment of military effort.

The entire program has been accomplished with an average of about 17 C-123 spray aircraft and several smaller helicopter sprayers plus some improvised ground spray equipment.

Herbicide operations are conducted under a program directed by the Government of South Vietnam. Requests for these operations generally originate at the district or provincial level and are submitted through territorial administration command channels. The herbicide spray plan includes as a minimum the area requested to be treated with herbicide, the public information, civil affairs and intelligence annexes, along with a statement by the province chief that he will see that just and legal claims are paid for any accidental damage. The ARVN corps commanders and their US corps senior advisors have been delegated authority to approve small scale defoliation by ground-based spray and by helicopters. All requests for crop destruction and larger scale defoliation by C-123 aircraft are forwarded to the Vietnamese Joint General Staff. Upon approval of the request by the Chief of Joint General Staff it is forwarded to the MACV staff for final review.

The MACV staff position is developed as the result of coordination with CORDS (Civil Operations and Revolutionary Development Support), USAID, and political representatives at each level where they exist. An aerial reconnaissance is conducted as the next step to ensure that all populated areas and friendly crops have been excluded from the target area. Having determined from this aerial survey and an analysis of the military worth that the project is a valid herbicide target, the project is forwarded to the US Ambassador and COMUSMACV for approval. The Ambassador personally approves all C-123 defoliation projects and all enemy crop destruction projects.

Some specific uses of herbicides are:

1. *Defoliation of Base Perimeters.*

A portion of the small scale ground based or the helicopter spray missions are used in improving the defense of base camps and fire bases. Herbicides are a great help in keeping down the growth of high jungle grass, bushes and weeds which will grow in cleared areas near these camps. This clearance opens fields of fire and affords observation for outposts to prevent surprise attack and as such is truly a life-saving measure for our forces and our allies. Without the use of herbicides around our fire bases, adequate defense is difficult and in many places impossible.

2. *Defoliation of Lines of Communication.*

There are many instances of ambush sites being defoliated for better aerial observation and improved visibility along roads and trails. In 1967 there were also many requests for defoliation of VC tax collection points. In otherwise friendly territory there were points along well travelled routes where the enemy could hide under cover and intercept travellers to demand taxes. Defoliation along these roads was very effective in opening these areas so that they can be seen from observation aircraft, and with few exceptions these roads were opened to free travel. The use of aircraft to spray alongside lines of communication proved valuable in clearing these areas and preventing costly ambush of army convoys with resulting friendly casualties.

3. *Defoliation of Infiltration Routes.*

Areas used by the enemy for routes of approach, resupply or movement are targets for herbicide spray. Probably the most valuable use of herbicides for defoliation is to permit aerial observation in such areas. This is particularly true in areas near the border so that we can detect movement of enemy units and their resupply.

4. *Defoliation of Enemy Base Camps.*

We know from prisoners of war and from observation that the enemy will move from areas that have been sprayed. Therefore, enemy base camps or unit headquarters are sprayed in order to make him move to avoid exposing himself to aerial observation. If he does move back in while the area is still defoliated, he will be observed and can be engaged.

5. *Crop Destruction.*

Crops in areas remote from the friendly population and known to belong to the enemy and which cannot be captured by ground operations are sometimes sprayed. Such targets are carefully selected so as to attack only those crops known to be grown by or for the VC or NVA. The authorization to attack crops in specific areas has been made by the US Embassy, Saigon, MACV and South Vietnamese Government.

Frequent reviews have been conducted of the Herbicide Program. The most recent one was personally directed and reviewed by COMUSMACV in October 1968 to assure himself that the program was militarily effective. Prior to that, the US Ambassador had directed a review which looked at the political and economic aspects of the program. The Embassy report was released in August 1968. The crop destruction program was also reviewed by the CINCPAC Scientific Advisor in December 1967. Each of these reports concluded that the program should be continued.

The requests for defoliation and crop destruction have always exceeded our capability to spray. The requirement continues although a tapering off should develop if enemy activity subsides. A recent review by MACV indicated that operations for 1970 will be less than in 1969. In addition, Rome plows are replacing defoliation for clearing along many lines of communication.

With regard to the recent publicity of the herbicide agent, 2,4,5-T, which is a component of orange, a herbicide mixture, the Bionetics Research Laboratories conducted a study of the carcinogenic, teratogenic and mutagenic activity of selected pesticides and industrial chemicals for the National Cancer Institute during the period 1965-1968. The study indicated that a large dose of 2,4,5-T administered orally to specific strains of mice during the central portion of the gestation period produced abnormal fetuses.

However, on 29 October 1969, Dr. DuBridge, Science Advisor to the President, stated, "It seems improbable that any person could receive harmful amounts of this chemical from any of the existing uses of 2,4,5-T."

Nevertheless, Deputy Secretary of Defense David Packard has issued instructions to the Joint Chiefs of Staff to re-emphasize the already existing policy that 2,4,5-T be utilized only in areas remote from population.

When the American Embassy conducted the political and economic review of the herbicide program, it requested that a disinterested expert be sent from the United States to assess any ecological consequences of the program. Dr. Fred Tschirley, Agricultural Research Service, Department of Agriculture, was sent over in March 1968 for a one-month period. Arrangements were made which permitted him to fly over any area of Vietnam he wished to inspect plus on-the-ground visits to any safe area. He concluded that the defoliation program had caused some ecological changes. Although single treatment on semideciduous forest would cause inconsequential changes, repeated treatments could kill enough trees to permit invasion of many sites by bamboo. The presence of bamboo would then retard regeneration of the forest.

The Army supports the need for a more detailed investigation of the ecological effects of herbicides used in Vietnam. Such an investigation should be conducted in coordination with other interested agencies. In order to get such a study started, a research and development project entitled "Ecological Effects of the Military Use of Herbicides in Vietnam" is being initiated. This study would continue into the post-hostilities phase.

In the final analysis the sole purpose of the herbicide program is to protect friendly forces and conserve manpower. The following examples should demonstrate the success of the defoliation effort in Vietnam:

1. Major defoliation has been accomplished in War Zone C. Prior to defoliation, 7 brigades were necessary to maintain US/GVN presence. During 1967, after defoliation only 3 brigades were required.

2. The Commander of Naval Forces in Vietnam in a report to General Abrams stated: "As you know, a major concern is the vegetation along the main shipping channel. Your continuing efforts under difficult and hazardous flying conditions, in keeping this area and the adjacent inland areas devoid of vegetation have contributed considerably

in denying the protective cover from which to ambush the slow-moving merchant ships and US Navy craft."

3. In 1968, the Commanding General of the First Field Force reported: "Defoliation has been effective in enhancing the success of allied combat operations. Herbicide operations using C-123 aircraft, helicopters, truck mounted and hand sprayers have become an integral part of the II CTZ operations against VC/NVA. The operations are normally limited to areas under VC/NVA control remote from population centers. The defoliation program has resulted in the reduction of enemy concealment and permitted increased use of supply routes by friendly units. Aerial surveillance of enemy areas has improved and less security forces are required to control areas of responsibility. An overall result of the herbicide program has been to increase friendly security and to assist in returning civilians to GVN control."

4. The US Commander in the III CTZ related: "Herbicide operations have contributed significantly to allied combat operations in the III Corps. Defoliation is an important adjunct to target acquisition. Aerial photographs can often be taken from which interpreters can 'see the ground' in areas that previously were obscured. Defoliation also aids visual reconnaissance. USAF FAC's (forward air controllers) and US Army aerial observers have discovered entire VC base camps in defoliated areas that had previously been overlooked."

5. In the south in the IV CTZ, C-123 herbicide operations are limited. This is because of the vast areas of valuable crops which are not to be destroyed, even though they may be in enemy hands. Therefore, the commander of the IV Corps area in presenting his evaluation cited the value of helicopter operations as follows: "A significant helicopter defoliation mission was conducted in the vicinity of SADEC in August 1968. The target area consisted of 3 main canals which converged and formed a strong VC base. The dense vegetation permitted visibility of only 10-15 meters hoizontally and nil vertically. The area was sprayed with approximately 735 gallons of herbicide White and over

90 percent of the area was defoliated. As the result of the defoliation, an ARVN battalion was able to remain overnight in the area for the first time in five years. Many enemy bunkers were open to observation. Since the defoliation, the VC presence has decreased to the point that only RF/PF forces are now necessary for local security."

6. As a part of the 1968 evaluation report of herbicide operations, the US Senior Advisor in the IV Corps Tactical Zone area reported: "A section of National Highway 4 in Phong Dinh Province was the site for a defoliation operation on 24 June 1968. Since January 1968, a series of ambushes was conducted against SVN convoys and troop movements. Because of the total inability of ground troops to keep the area clear of VC, this area was sprayed using 685 gallons of herbicide White. The target area was primarily coconut palm and banana trees that had been abandoned by their owners for several years. During the period of abandonment the vegetation had become so dense that convoy security elements were not able to see more than five meters into the underbrush and had to rely on reconnaissance by fire to discover the hidden enemy. This method of protection had proven ineffective. Three RF/PF companies with US advisors were used to secure the target for the helicopter operation in addition to an armored cavalry troop. Since the defoliation mission was completed, convoys have used the highway 2 or 3 times a week without attack or harassment. Only one RF platoon has remained in the area to provide local security to the hamlet and highway."

7. In certain instances, we know the VC have been forced to divert tactical units from combat missions to food-procurement operations and food-transportation tasks, attesting to the effectiveness of the crop destruction program. In local areas where extensive crop destruction missions were conducted, VC/NVA defections to GVN increased as a result of low morale resulting principally from food shortages.

The most highly valued item of equipment to field commanders in Vietnam is the helicopter. There was some question when the helicopter spray equipment was first procured whether field commanders would divert the use of helicopters from combat operations for herbicide spray operations. The very fact that the commanders have used their helicopter spray equipment to the fullest and have asked for more is certainly proof that herbicide operations have been helpful in protecting the American soldier and contributing to successful accomplishment of the ground combat mission.

DuBridge Statement

Executive Office of the President
Office of Science and Technology

October 29, 1969

Dr. Lee A. DuBridge, Science Adviser to the President and Executive Secretary of the President's Environmental Quality Council, announced today a coordinated series of actions that are being taken by the agencies of Government to restrict the use of the weed-killing chemical, 2,4,5-T.

The actions to control the use of the chemical were taken as a result of findings from a laboratory study conducted by Bionetics Research Laboratories which indicated that offspring of mice and rats given relatively large oral doses of the herbicide during early stages of pregnancy showed a higher than expected number of deformities.

Although it seems improbable that any person could receive harmful amounts of this chemical from any of the existing uses of 2,4,5-T, and while the relationships of these effects in laboratory animals to effects in man are not entirely clear at this time, the actions taken will assure safety of the public while further evidence is being sought.

The study involved relatively small numbers of laboratory rats and mice. More extensive studies are needed and will be undertaken. At best it is difficult to extrapolate results obtained with laboratory animals to man—sensitivity to a given compound may be different in man than in animal species; metabolic pathways may be different.

2,4,5-T is highly effective in control of many species of broad-leaf weeds and woody plants, and is used on ditch banks, along roadsides, on rangelands, and other places. Almost none is used by home gardeners or in residential areas. The chemical is effective in defoliating trees and shrubs and its use in South Vietnam has resulted in reducing greatly the number of ambushes, thus saving lives. The following actions are being taken:

The Department of Agriculture will cancel registrations of 2,4,5-T for use on food crops effective January 1, 1970, unless by that time the Food and Drug Administration has found a basis for establishing a safe legal tolerance in and on foods.

The Department of Health, Education, and Welfare will complete action on the petition requesting a finite tolerance for 2,4,5-T residues on foods prior to January 1, 1970.

The Departments of Agriculture and Interior will stop use in their own programs of 2,4,5-T in populated areas or where residues from use could otherwise reach man.

The Department of Defense will restrict the use of 2,4,5-T to areas remote from the population.

Other Departments of the Government will take such actions in their own programs as may be consistent with these announced plans.

The Department of State will advise other countries of the actions being taken by the United States to protect the health of its citizens and will make available to such countries the technical data on which these decisions rest.

Appropriate Departments of Government will undertake immediately to verify and extend the available experimental evidence so as to provide the best technical basis possible for such future actions as the Government might wish to undertake with respect to 2,4,5-T and similar compounds.

Statement by the President on Biological Defense Policies and Programs

The White House

November 25, 1969

Soon after taking office I directed a comprehensive study of our chemical and biological defense policies and programs. There had been no such review in over fifteen years. As a result, objectives and policies in this field were unclear and programs lacked definition and direction.

Under the auspices of the National Security Council, the Departments of State and Defense, the Arms Control and Disarmament Agency, the Office of Science and Technology, the Intelligence Community and other agencies worked closely together on this study for over six months. These government efforts were aided by contributions from the scientific community through the President's Scientific Advisory Committee.

This study has now been completed and its findings carefully considered by the National Security Council. I am now reporting the decisions taken on the basis of this review.

CHEMICAL WARFARE PROGRAM

As to our chemical warfare program, the United States:
Reaffirms its oft-repeated renunciation of the first use of lethal chemical weapons.

Extends this renunciation to the first use of incapacitating chemicals.

Consonant with these decisions, the Administration will submit to the Senate, for its advice and consent to ratification, The Geneva Protocol of 1925 which prohibits the first use in war of "asphyxiating, poisonous or other Gases and of Bacteriological Methods of Warfare." The United States has long supported the principles and objectives of this Protocol. We take this step toward formal ratification to reinforce our continuing advocacy of international constraints on the use of these weapons.

BIOLOGICAL RESEARCH PROGRAM

Biological weapons have massive, unpredictable and potentially uncontrollable consequences. They may produce global epidemics and impair the health of future generations. I have therefore decided that:

The U.S. shall renounce the use of lethal biological agents and weapons, and all other methods of biological warfare.

The U.S. will confine its biological research to defensive measures such as immunization and safety measures.

The DOD has been asked to make recommendations as to the disposal of existing stocks of bacteriological weapons.

In the spirit of these decisions, the United States associates itself with the principles and objectives of the United Kingdom Draft Convention which would ban the use of Biological methods of warfare. We will seek, however, to clarify specific provisions of the draft to assure that necessary safeguards are included.

Neither our association with the Convention nor the limiting of our program to research will leave us vulnerable to surprise by an enemy who does not observe these rational restraints. Our intelligence community will continue to watch carefully the nature and extent of the biological programs of others.

These important decisions, which have been announced today, have been taken as an initiative toward peace. Mankind already carries in its own hands too many of the seeds of its own destruction. By the examples we set today, we hope to contribute to an atmosphere of peace and understanding between nations and among men.

Resolution Passed by the Council of the American Association For the Advancement of Science

December 30, 1969
Boston, Massachusetts

Whereas, recent studies commissioned by the National Cancer Institute have shown that 2,4,5-T and 2,4-D cause birth malformations in experimental animals, and

Whereas, the above studies conclude that 2,4,5-T is probably dangerous to man, and that 2,4-D is potentially dangerous to man, and

Whereas, 2,4,5-T and 2,4-D are widely used for military defoliation in Vietnam in amounts (20 to 30 lbs/acre) that are much greater than those used in civilian operations, and

Whereas, there is a possibility that the use of herbicides in Vietnam is causing birth malformations among infants of exposed mothers;

Therefore, be it resolved that the Council of AAAS urge that the U.S. Department of Defense immediately cease all use of 2,4-D and 2,4,5-T in Vietnam.

Statement by the AAAS Herbicide Assessment Commission,

December 28, 1969

The American Association for the Advancement of Science has asked Dr. Matthew S. Meselson of Harvard University to plan a study of the effects of the military use of herbicides and defoliants on the ecology and on human welfare in Vietnam. Dr. Meselson will be assisted by Dr. Arthur H. Westing, currently on leave from Windham College, Putney, Vermont, where he is Chairman of the Department of Biology.

Preliminary plans for the design of the study are as follows: after a brief initial period of reading and inquiry, a document will be drafted identifying the questions to be answered by the proposed study. This document will be circulated for comments to a group of specialists and other interested persons, then revised to form a working paper which will guide the design of the study. A design for a study which will provide answers to the questions posed in the working paper will then be drafted and similarly circulated and revised. At that point, a summer conference will be held to bring together a commission of specialists. This conference will discuss, revise, and expand the preliminary design, which will later be circulated once more for comments, then revised to form the final design for a study. Designs for alternative long-term and short-term studies will be prepared, as the conditions under which a study may finally be carried out are still unknown. The design should be finished before the end of 1970. Sometime in the course of the work, a trip to Vietnam for preliminary study is likely to be necessary.

Military Use of Herbicides

**A Tentative List of Questions
for Possible Investigation**

AAAS Herbicide Assessment Commission

Botanical Museum, Harvard University
Cambridge, Massachusetts 02138, U.S.A.

I. THE HERBICIDES

A. *Usage of Herbicides*

1. What are the major chemicals that have been used? Where have they been used? At what times? At what dosages? How many repetitions? In what total quantities?

2. To what extent have herbicides affected regions not intended to be sprayed? By flight errors and accidents? By drift? By volatilization? By transport in water?

3. What is the purity of the chemicals used? What are the levels of possibly significant contaminants? How has this varied in each major lot?

4. What findings and what claims are already available regarding effects of herbicides in South Vietnam (or in relevant situations elsewhere)?

5. Are there countermeasures or antidotes that can be applied to ameliorate any adverse effects of the chemicals used? Are any being used?

B. *Fate of Herbicides after Application*

6. At what rates and by what processes do herbicides

disappear from the soil in the different habitat types in which they are used? from the water? from living organisms? What is the situation in areas sprayed once or more than once?

7. What are the specific chemical and biochemical pathways of herbicide decomposition? Do these differ in the different habitat types involved?

8. What important abnormal metabolites or abnormal metabolite levels does herbicide application induce in living organisms?

9. Does the burning of wood or leaves from herbicide treated vegetation produce any significantly harmful products?

10. What levels of herbicides, herbicide breakdown products, and herbicide induced substances are ingested by various human population groups?

II. ECOLOGY

A. Baseline Data

1. What are the major natural vegetational types (communities) in South Vietnam, and what is their species composition? How are the types distributed, and what is their extent?

2. At approximately what successional stage is each type? What are the presumed successional states for each type?

3. What is the composition of the animal communities that accompany each of the vegetational types?

4. What are the major soil types and their distribution?

5. What are the climatological conditions?

B. Effects of Herbicide Usage

6. What plant and animal species are particularly sensitive to the different herbicides (or contaminants or breakdown products)? Why?

7. How do the several plant communities change following one spraying? Several sprayings?

8. How do the associated animal communities change?

9. How do the soil macro- and micro-organisms change?

10. How have the aquatic habitats (as well as the edible fish, etc.) been affected?

11. Are any of the soil types affected? In texture or structure? In organic-matter content of the litter layer or below? In nutrient availability? Has significant erosion or laterization resulted? Are there changes in the water table?

12. What are the important specific effects on the plants and animals exposed to the herbicides? Are there significant effects on health? growth? development? fecundity? chromosomes?

13. Are there significant ecological interactions between herbicide effects and bomb craters, bulldozing, fire, etc.?

III. HEALTH (PUBLIC AND INDIVIDUAL)

A. *Baseline Data*

1. What was the population distribution in South Vietnam before 1960? For each year since?

2. Are there other basic demographic data available for these years on a region by region basis?

3. Are there detailed public health data available for each of the years and regions of interest?

4. Are there disease vector data available (population sizes and distributions)?

5. What have been the public health measures routinely employed for the years and in the regions of interest?

6. Where are the major hospitals in South Vietnam and by whom are they operated?

B. *Effects of Herbicide Usage*

Note: The following questions apply to the herbicides themselves as well as to their contaminants and breakdown products, and to deleterious induced metabolites possibly produced in food organisms subjected to spraying.

7. Are there significant immediate (or acute) threats to

human health from direct contact with or ingestion of
the chemicals involved? What proportion of the population is particularly (or abnormally) susceptible or al-
lergic to each of the chemicals involved?

8. Are there significant long-range (or chronic) threats
to humans? Toxicity? Teratogenesis? Carcinogenesis?
Mutagenesis?

9. What is the extent and seriousness of malnutrition that
can be attributed to herbicide usage?

10. Are any of the possible health problems related in
severity to age, sex, previous medical history, or other
factors?

IV. HUMAN WELFARE (SOCIAL AND ECONOMIC)

A. *Baseline Data*

1. What are the living standards of rural South Vietnamese in unsprayed regions in the various parts of
South Vietnam (or in affected areas, prior to spraying)?

2. What is the structure of the rural local economy in
unsprayed regions in the various parts of South Vietnam
(or in affected areas, prior to spraying)?

Note: See also questions III.1 and 2.

B. *Effects of Herbicide Usage*

3. What is the economic impact on local populations of
one spraying? of several sprayings? What is the impact
on individuals; on the village economy; on local markets?

4. How (and how permanently) are garden crops affected? Tree fruits? Livestock?

5. How (and how permanently) are orchards and plantations affected? Rubber; coffee; tea; kapok; teak; etc.?

6. How (and how permanently) is fishing affected?

7. How (and how permanently) is forestry affected? For
timber; pulp; charcoal; game; etc.?

8. What is the psychological impact of herbicide usage?

9. To what extent does herbicide usage contribute to

population migration? What proportion of this migration is permanent? What are the resulting urban and
other social effects?

10. Are there beneficial effects from spraying?

11. Are there ameliorative measures that should be (and
can be) instituted to mitigate herbicidal damage? At the
time of spraying? Afterwards?

V. PROCEDURES AND PRIORITIES

1. Of all the questions listed, which are of highest pri-
ority?

2. Are there additional important questions which have
been overlooked?

3. Which of the questions are likely to be answerable in
one year? two years? five years?

4. What would be the optimal staffing, equipment, and
facility requirements in the answering of these questions?
What would be the minimal requirements?

5. Whose cooperation must or should be sought in attempting to answer these questions?

Statement of Dr. Arthur W. Galston, Professor of Biology and Lecturer in Forestry, Yale University

---

Delivered before the Subcommittee on National Security Policy and Scientific Developments of the Committee on Foreign Affairs House of Representatives

December, 1969

Mr. GALSTON. Thank you, Mr. Chairman. I apologize for my late arrival, and also for not having a prepared statement. I was informed of this hearing just a few days ago, and have not had the opportunity to prepare one.

Mr. ZABLOCKI. Very good, sir.

Mr. GALSTON. I will, however, make some extemporaneous statements, with the aid of notes, if I might.

Mr. ZABLOCKI. You may proceed, Doctor.

USE OF HERBICIDES AS WEAPONS

Mr. GALSTON. I am a botanist, and I would like to confine my remarks to the use of herbicides as military weapons in Vietnam, with some overtones concerning the social and health implications of their use in the United States.

Since 1962, about 4 million acres of Vietnam have been sprayed with about 100 million pounds of assorted herbicides. This is an area about the size of the State of Massachusetts.

The agents which have been used in Vietnam may be classed into three types of chemicals: The first type, Agent Orange, consists of two commonly used phenoxyacetic acids that go by the shorthand names of 2,4-D and 2,4,5-T.

They are used in Vietnam at about 27 pounds per acre, and I should say parenthetically that this is up to 10 times the usual domestic dose recommended.

Agent White is a mixture of 2,4-D and a fairly new chemical called picloram or tordon. This mixture is sprayed so as to deposit about 6 pounds of 2,4-D and 1½ pounds of picloram per acre.

The third agent, called Agent Blue, is known chemically as cacodylic acid. It is an arsenic-containing material, and is sprayed at the rate of about 9.3 pounds per acre.

As Mr. Swyter has already mentioned, the main object of our use of these chemicals is to defoliate around trails, estuaries and encampments to prevent ambush, infiltration and military buildups. By all odds, this use of these chemicals appears to have been militarily successful.

A secondary use has to do mainly with cacodylic acid, a chemical uniquely adapted to kill grass plants such as rice. We spray and kill rice in paddies of outlying areas which are suspected of being supply centers for bands of guerrillas. In some instances entire villages are suspected of being Vietcong sympathizers; killing their food crops prevents their use as a staging area for any sort of military operations and has in some instances led to complete abandonment of the village.

All of these chemicals are in use in the United States. Their use was initiated on a large scale at about the end of World War II. In fact, 2,4-D and its relative 2,4,5-T were developed in what is now known as Fort Detrick. The early formulations were made there, and the use of these chemicals as agriculturally important herbicides and plant growth regulators stemmed in part from those early military investigations.

It has been assumed, because of the rapid breakdown of

2,4-D in the soil, that the massive use of this chemical does not constitute a health hazard. I shall have occasion to return to this point, because recent evidence indicates that not only 2,4-D, but more importantly, its relative 2,4,5-T, may constitute an important health hazard, both at home and in Vietnam.

UNDERSCORE EFFECTS OF HERBICIDE USE

The kinds of undesirable consequences that flow from our massive use of herbicides can be summarized under three general headings. Some of these have been already alluded to briefly by Mr. Swyter, and I hope I may enlarge on them.

One is ecological damage; the second would be inadvertent agricultural damage, and the third involves direct damage to people.

I. ECOLOGICAL DAMAGE

Under ecological damage, it has already been well documented that some kinds of plant associations subject to spray, especially by Agent Orange, containing 2,4-D and 2,4,5-T, have been irreversibly damaged. I refer specifically to the mangrove associations that line the estuaries, especially around the Saigon River.

Up to 100,000 acres of these mangroves have been sprayed. In a report published in *Science* about a year ago,[1] Dr. Fred Tschirley, who went to Vietnam at the behest of the U.S. State Department, confirmed that there was extensive killing of these mangrove associations by one spray of 2,4-D. Some of them had been sprayed as early as 1961 and have shown no substantial signs of recovery. Ecologists have estimated a minimum of 20-25 years for effective recovery to occur.

You might ask why we should be concerned with the mangrove associations. What are they to us? Ecologists have known for a long time that the mangroves lining estuaries furnish one of the most important ecological niches for the completion of the life cycle of certain shellfish and migratory fish. If these plant communities are not in a

[1]Tschirley, F. H., "Defoliation in Vietnam," Science 163: 779-786, 1969.

healthy state, secondary effects on the whole interlocked web of organisms are bound to occur.

So not only is there now likely to be increased erosion along the estuaries, and destruction of that stable environment, but in the years ahead the Vietnamese, who do not have overabundant sources of proteins anyhow, are probably going to suffer dietarily because of the deprivation of food in the form of fish and shellfish. I would assume that the United States will have to assume the major responsibility for making up the deficiency.

DAMAGE TO SOIL

Damage to the soil is another possible consequence of extensive defoliation. It has been minimized by some, but I think we will find, when we look at Vietnam in detail after hostilities are over, that there has been considerable damage done to the soil in various parts of the country. I state this firmly, as a conviction which I have as a botanist.

We know that the soil is not a dead, inert mass, but, rather, that it is a vibrant, living community. Up to one-half of the total weight of some soils can be micro-organisms who derive their food from the organic matter excreted from the fine roots of trees and other vegetation growing in any area. If you knock the leaves off of trees once, twice or three times, whether you kill them or not, you interfere with the excretion of organic matter into the soil; you cause an alteration in the level of activity of these microbes; you change the quality of the soil.

We know from our own soils that microbes are important in that they synthesize gummy substances which cement the soil particles together. This gives us the crumb structure that the agriculturalist knows is essential for good tilth, with good aeration, good water- and mineral-holding capacity and good quality for the growth of roots. Failing the microbial activity, we could have compaction of soil particles into hard clays, into which roots have difficulty penetrating. If this occurs agricultural productivity declines markedly, and recovery may be a very slow process.

Worse than this, certain tropical soils—and it has been estimated that in Vietnam up to 50 percent of all the soils fall into this category—are laterizable; that is, they may be irreversibly converted to rock as a result of their deprivation of organic matter. Many tropical soils are very weak in what the agriculturalist knows as base exchange capacity. The only thing that stabilizes the soil is its organic matter. If, as I have mentioned earlier, you deprive trees of their leaves and photosynthesis stops, organic matter in the soil declines and laterization, the making of brick, may occur on a very extensive scale. I would emphasize that this brick is irreversibly hardened; it cannot be made back into soil, short of breaking it up with a sledge hammer or similar device. Part of the Temple of Angkor Wat in Cambodia is made of laterized soil. The fact that this temple has been around for 11 centuries is a testimonial to the persistence of such material.

Another ecological consequence is the invasion of an area by undesirable plants. One of the main plants that invades an area that has been defoliated is bamboo. Bamboo is one of the most difficult of all plants to destroy once it becomes established where you don't want it. It is not amenable to killing by herbicides. Frequently it has to be burned over, and this causes tremendous dislocations to agriculture.

DANGERS OF PICLORAM

Finally, in the line of ecological damage, I would note that the recently introduced chemical picloram is one of the longest lived pesticides I know of in soil. I believe it to be a herbicidal analog of DDT. As we all know, DDT, introduced into our ecosystem, persists for years and years. Picloram is not quite that long lived, but it is very long lived, indeed, compared with any other herbicide.

In "Down to Earth," a publication of the Dow Chemical Co., which synthesizes this material, I have read that less than 3½ percent of the applied picloram disappeared from certain California clay soils in a field trial lasting 467 days.

In other soils, the disappearance is up to 20 percent of the applied material in 467 days.

It is clear that picloram, once applied, could be around for years. I would suggest that its massive application to the soils of Vietnam is going to hamper agriculture, even after hostilities are over, for some time into the future.

II. INADVERTENT AGRICULTURAL DAMAGE

My second category of damage is inadvertent agricultural damage. There are many useful plants growing in all parts of South Vietnam. When one flies over a forested area that one wishes to defoliate, with a converted cargo plane carrying tanks of herbicidal liquid delivered through high-pressure nozzles, one hopes that one has gaged the meteorological situation accurately and that the fine droplets produced by these nozzles will, in fact, fall on areas whose spraying is desired.

It is understandable, weather being what it is, that winds come up occasionally, that meteorological patterns change drastically, and that pilots miss the mark. All sorts of inadvertent accidents can happen. Finishing a run with some gallons left in the tank, and jettisoning the rest, may cause it to fall in areas not desired, as the Skull Valley accident made dramatically clear.

We have documentation of several very important accidents of this kind in Vietnam. For example, thousands of trees in the Michelin rubber plantation to the north and west of Saigon were injured a few years ago following a spray operation. Some trees were killed, some recovered slowly, but the United States has compensated the French owners of that rubber plantation at the rate of $87 per tree.

In Cambodia, we are now facing a lawsuit by the Cambodian Government to the extent of about $9 million, resulting from extensive spraying in the Tay Ninh Province of neighboring South Vietnam. The report of the investigation team, which included Dr. Fred H. Tschirley and Dr. Charles Minarik of Fort Detrick, concluded that only a part of the damage is due to inadvertent drift. Some damage appears to have been due to deliberate spraying over the Cambodian border. In any event some 700 square kilometers of territory were affected, and the outcome of this lawsuit is still to be determined.

There have been documented reports of extensive damage to truck crops grown along roads, trails, and canals near Saigon. This results, I believe, from the drifting of herbicide from regions where they were intended to be deposited, over to areas in which truck farms were being cultivated. I believe the extent of this damage has not been accurately calculated, but certainly must go into the millons of dollars.

III. DAMAGE TO PEOPLE

Finally, I would like to discuss the most recent danger of the use of these herbicides to come to light. I refer to their direct damage to people. It is a source of great distress to me to find that some 25 years after the first introduction of the chlorinated phenoxyacetic acids like 2,4-D and 2,4,5-T, which together constitute about a $40 million business in this country today, that there have not been published before this year adequate toxicological data to support their extensive use in agriculture.

We have depended upon the fact that 2,4-D is rapidly degraded in soil by micro-organisms. We usually say its half-life is just a few weeks. 2,4,5-T, with just one extra chlorine atom on the benzene ring, is substantially longer lived. It is this chemical which has now been shown to be harmful to animals, although 2,4-D is also suspect.

About 2 years ago, a toxicological study was commissioned by the National Institutes of Health, and carried out by a private research organization called the Bionetics Research Laboratory in Bethesda, Md.

Three kinds of tests were made on a large number of commonly used agricultural chemicals. One involved mutagenicity; that is, do the chemicals cause mutations? This test was carried out against micro-organisms. Second, are the chemicals carcinogenic? Do they produce cancers when injected into test organisms such as mice? Thirdly, are they teratogenic; that is, do they cause malformations in developing embryos?

TERATOGENIC EFFECTS OF 2,4,5-T

The teratogenic chemical with which most of us are familiar is, of course, thalidomide. It has recently been divulged that 2,4,5-T is one of the most teratogenic chemicals known. In experiments by the Bionetics Laboratory in which 2,4,5-T was fed in the diet, in honey, from 4.6 up to 113 milligrams per kilogram body weight, extensive teratogenic damage was noted. Even at the lowest dose I have quoted, 4.6 milligrams per kilogram, there was marked enlargement of the liver of the mother. This shows that the body was trying to cope with this extra burden, trying to detoxify the chemical which was applied. This dose also produced a significant rise in abnormal births in rats.

If the chemical was injected subcutaneously, the damage was somewhat greater. At the highest concentration used, 113 milligrams per kilogram body weight, which is equivalent to only a few ounces, for a human, 100 percent of all of the litters born had at least one abnormality, and up to 70 percent of all the offspring were abnormal in some major respect.

The abnormalities include lack of heads, lack of eyes, faulty eyes, cystic kidneys, cleft palate, enlarged livers, and other types of damage which toxicologists and teratologists feel are very significant.

The results with mice were so striking that tests were conducted with rats, and the rat tests confirmed the teratogenicity. I suppose the next step will be to test this chemical in rabbits, dogs, and then in primates.

When the President's science adviser, Dr. DuBridge, was made aware of these results, he issued an order which restrained the use of 2,4,5-T, both domestically and in Vietnam. As I understand it, as of the 1st of January 1970, 2-4,5-T, which is used massively domestically will not be available for agricultural usage, and its use will be restricted to clearing the underbrush from around powerlines, railway embankments, and the like. In Vietnam, its use in populated areas is to be discontinued. The Department of Defense has announced that this is consistent with present use, and that operations involving 2,4,5-T will proceed as before.

I suggest that its teratogenicity is such that even its use in such apparently innocuous domestic manners as clearing brush near powerlines is undesirable. Such chemicals could find their ways into water supplies, and could be ingested in teratogenic doses.

EFFECTS OF 2,4,5-T IN VIETNAM

We have sprayed 2,4,5-T exhaustively in Vietnam. Have we caused any damage to people there? One can't know for sure. All that one can do is put together various bits of evidence. We know that 27 pounds per acre are sprayed. Let us assume that 2,4-D is completely nontoxic, although the Bionetics report indicates that it, too, is suspect, and should be further investigated.

If you consider only the 2,4,5-T sprayed and assume that a 1-inch rainfall, which is quite common in South Vietnam, has occurred after the spray, then you can calculate that there are about 50 milligrams per liter of 2,4,5-T in the water. Most of the drinking water and cooking water in South Vietnam is gathered in two ways—either from very shallow wells, or from catching the rainwater from the rooftops and keeping it in cisterns.

If one assumes that a pregnant woman drinks a liter of water a day, which is certainly conservative, then she consumes about 1½ milligrams per kilo of body weight per day. While this is a little bit below the lowest level tested in the Bionetics survey, I would recall to you that even those lowest levels indicated some damage in the form of oversized livers and abnormal births. Furthermore we cannot be sure that humans are not more sensitive to the 2,4,5-T than are these test animals.

I would also like to suggest that if the rainfall were less

or water consumption more or if there were uneven deposits of 2,4,5-T, then significant teratogenic events could have occurred among Vietnamese women.

REPORTS OF ABNORMAL BIRTHS FROM SAIGON

Is there any evidence that such damage has occurred? If one looks at the Saigon newspapers, one finds that since late 1967, which would coincide with the end of the first year of our massive spray operations, there have been numerous reports, in the Saigon newspapers, of the incidence, especially in two hospitals in Saigon, of a completely new kind of birth abnormality. It is called the "egg bundle-like fetus," pictures of which have been published on the front pages of some of the Saigon newspapers.

We do not know, of course, what is causing these abnormal births. There are many traumatic events occurring in South Vietnam, and we cannot say that 2,4,5-T is the trauma which is giving rise to these abnormal births. But I would say that the entire spectrum of events compels me, as a biologist, to examine current restrictions on the use of all of these chemicals, none of which has been tested adequately for effects on humans and animals close to humans. I would hope that further restrictions would be placed on the use of these chemicals until we are sure that they are not causing adverse effects on people at home as well as in Vietnam.

Like Mr. Swyter, I would hope that the herbicides would be included in those "asphyxiating, poisonous, and other gases and analogous liquids, materials, and devices" whose use is banned in the Geneva Protocol, which will shortly be resubmitted to the Senate for ratification.

I would hope that the Senate, and all others concerned with this problem would do all they can, in the light of the evidence which I have presented, to include herbicides in the ban.

Report on Herbicidal Damage by the United States in Southeastern Cambodia

By A. H. Westing, E. W. Pfeiffer, J. Lavorel, & L. Matarasso

Phnom Penh
December 31, 1969

INTRODUCTION

This is a preliminary report of a study of herbicidal damage by the United States in southeastern Cambodia carried out by an *ad hoc* international scientific commission. It is based upon four days of intensive field investigation during the period of 25 to 29 December 1969 and upon additional detailed interviews in Phnom Penh with M. Chuon Saodi, the Cambodian Minister of Agriculture, M. Min Sarim, the Director General of State Rubber Plantations, M. Suon Kaset, the Director of Waters, Forests, and Game, M. Hing Un, Director of Agriculture, M. Sor Thay Seng, Chief of the Division of Agronomy, and with other government officials.

Our study was made possible by the Royal Government of Cambodia, which supplied us with all land and air transportation and other help necessary to visit the areas

117

in question and to otherwise perform our mission. Any and all areas we wished to visit were freely open to us for purposes of inspection, interviewing, and photography.

In the field we were at all times accompanied by one or more scientists and occasionally other officials of the Cambodian government (and by an armed guard while working along the Vietnamese border). We received full coöperation and gracious hospitality wherever we went from the people at all levels of responsibility and in all walks of life. There was virtually no language barrier since French (and often English) was understood almost everywhere and since a Cambodian (Khmer) interpreter was always available to us as needed for communication with uneducated local inhabitants. M. Min Sarim, Director General of State Rubber Plantations (and a professional forester), accompanied us virtually at all times. He was most useful to us because of his close familiarity with most of the areas we visited and because of his knowledge of rubber culture, of forestry, and of agronomy. M. Min had studied for five years at the University of Quebec; he speaks Cambodian, French, and English.

It was our mission to make an independent scientific evaluation of the herbicidal damage done by the United States in April and May of 1969. One of our aims was to verify the earlier Cambodian and United States assessments of damage. We wished particularly to assess rate of recovery, extent of long-term effects, and the impact on the local inhabitants and their economy. A more general aim was to gain some preliminary insights into the ecological and economic damages caused by herbicidal chemical warfare in the light of its massive use by the United States in neighboring South Vietnam.

We had available to us the following reports relevant to the herbicidal incursions into Cambodia:

1. "A Grave Attack on the Cambodian Economy: Ravages Caused by the Defoliants Spread by American Aircraft near the Frontier." [a popular account]
   In: *Kambuja,* Vol. 5, No. 50, pp. 112-113, May 1969
2. "Rapport du Comité Chargé du Constat et de l'Evalu-

ation des Dégâts Dûs aux Epandages des Produits Dé-
foliants par les Avions Américano-Sudvietnamiens."
By Min Sarim *et al.* (an *ad hoc* Cambodian Ministry
of Agriculture committee)
Phnom Penh, 16 May 1969, 15 pp.
Plus three brief subsequent reports by this committee
of 10 July 1969 (5 pp.), 17 November 1969 (3 pp.),
and 9 December 1969 (4 pp.).
3. "A Report on Herbicide Damage to Rubber and Fruit
Trees in Cambodia."
By C. E. Minarik *et al.* (an *ad hoc* U. S. State Department team)
Saigon, 12 July 1969, 16 pp. + 5 appendixes [limited
distribution in November 1969]

PERSONNEL

The present study was conducted by a four-man *ad hoc*
scientific commission, two members from France and two
members from the United States:
1. JEAN LAVOREL (plant biophysicist)
Directeur de Recherche et Directeur du Laboratoire de
Photosynthèse du Centre National de la Recherche
Scientifique (CNRS)
91, Gif-Sur-Yvette, France
2. LÉON MATARASSO (lawyer)
Avocat à la Cour de Paris
Vice-Président du Centre International pour la Dénun-
ciation des Crimes de Guerre
29, Rue de Tournon, Paris, 6°, France
3. EGBERT W. PFEIFFER (Ph.D.; animal physiologist)
Professor of Zoology, University of Montana, Missoula,
Montana 59801, U.S.A.
4. ARTHUR H. WESTING (M.F., Ph.D.; plant physiolo-
gist)
Associate Professor of Botany & Chairman of Biology,
Windham College
Putney, Vermont 05346, U.S.A.

Field Itinerary

Thursday, 25 December 1969. Aerial examination by small reconnaissance plane of both damaged and undamaged rubber plantations and other lands. This was primarily over the undamaged Chup area and over the damaged areas of Krek, Chalang (Chalong), Mimot, (Mémot) and vicinity —all in the southeastern border province of Kompong Cham (adjacent to the South Vietnamese province of Tay Ninh).

Friday, 26 December 1969. Visit to the Cambodian Rubber Research Institute (Institut des Recherches sur le Caoutchouc au Cambodge; IRCC) at Chup and to the adjacent French rubber plantation (Compagnie du Cambodge). At IRCC we examined Institute records and interviewed the following professional staff:

Dr. W. L. Resing (chemist) (Director)
M. Gilbert Deconinck (plant pathologist)
M. Chai Kim Chun (biochemist)
M. Langlois (agronomist)
M. Tupy (plant physiologist)

We visited the adjacent plantation (the second largest in the world) in order to become acquainted with healthy rubber trees of the several major varieties at various ages.

Saturday, 27 December 1969. Visit to a moderately damaged, medium-sized, private (coöperative) plantation at Chipeang (just east of Krek) (employing *ca.* 500 workers), and to the associated village (population *ca.* 1,500). This was a typical (though somewhat larger) example of the many small plantations in the region that were damaged to a greater or lesser extent. We inspected the damage and interviewed M. Buoy San, the director, as well as several tappers and villagers at random.

Next, we visited the heavily damaged, large, private plantation at Dar (Société Khmère d'Hévéaculture de Dar; SKHD) in the company of Dr. Resing and M. Deconinck of IRCC. Here we also inspected the damage and interviewed M. Som Khom, the director, as well as several field foremen and tappers.

Monday, 29 December 1969. Visit to the rather heavily damaged, large French plantation at Mimot (Société des Plantations Réunies de Mimot; SPRM) which employs some 15,000 workers. Here we inspected the damage and interviewed:

M. E. Pellegrin (Director General)

M. C. Audureau (Assistant Director)

Dr. Charles Bosquet (M.D.; Director of the hospital at Mimot)

as well as the five Cambodian owners of five very small nearby rubber plantations (and each living in a different nearby village).

Next, we visited a small village in the vicinity (Chalang III) to inspect in some detail the damage done to local agricultural and horticultural crops and to interview the inhabitants.

OBSERVATIONS AND FINDINGS

General. The principal period of herbicidal application seems to have occurred during April and the early part of May of 1969, and thus at the end of the dry, dormant season. Our observations were therefore carried out some eight months later and after the passing of one complete growing season (the wet monsoon season of May through November). The U. S. State Department examination had been made about two months after spraying, shortly after the onset of the growing season.

About 70,000 hectares (173,000 acres) were damaged, of which about 10,000 hectares (24,700 acres) were damaged rather heavily. This affected area contains about 15,500 hectares (38,300 acres) of damaged rubber plantations, of which about 6,000 hectares (14,800 acres) were damaged rather heavily. Of the 15,500 hectares of damaged rubber, about 11,400 hectares (28,200 acres) are over 6-7 years old and thus in production.

The herbicides used seemed to have been restricted to

a mixture of 2,4-dichlorophenoxyacetic acid (2,4-D) and 2,4,5-trichlorophenoxyacetic acid (2,4,5-T) in oil soluble formulations; this mixture goes under the U. S. Defense Department code name "Orange." We concluded that it was agent Orange because of the characteristic, dramatic and selective effects of this hormonal class of herbicides; and because the essentially normal growth of the subsequently planted garden crops precluded the other more persistent agents also used by the U. S. armed forces. The severity and selectivity of injury suggested applications in the approximate range of 0.5 to 3 kilograms per hectare (0.4-3 pounds/acre) of active herbicidal ingredients. The lesser amount refers to the eastern and western portions of the affected area, the greater amount to the central portion.

The herbicidal mixture that was presumably used is highly (though somewhat variably) toxic to a wide range of dicotyledonous annuals and perennials, both herbaceous and woody (including rubber, numerous fruit, and some timber trees and many vegetables). It is generally less toxic to monocotyledonous plants (including rice and other cereals, bamboo, banana, and palms). Both 2,4-D and 2,4,5-T are toxic to lethal by virtue of being absorbed and translocated by the vegetation, thence to mimic certain natural endogenous growth hormones. They cause erratic and uncontrolled overgrowth, flower, fruit, and leaf abscission, branch dieback, temporary sterility, and other ill effects; and in some instances death. Any 2,4-D that reaches the ground decomposes within a few weeks after application, any 2,4,5-T within a few months.

Damage to rubber trees. Highly accurate damage estimates can be made with respect to rubber (*Hevea brasiliensis*) since very precise records are kept by the IRCC and the larger plantations on a variety by variety and block by block basis with respect to tree growth, tree health, latex yield, and latex quality. The managerial plantation personnel are well trained and competent, and the methods employed by them are scientifically and technologically up to date. Latex yield per hectare in this region is the highest in the world.

Although quite a number of varieties (clones *sensu stricto*) are in use in Cambodia, more than 90% of all commercial production is more or less equally based upon three major varieties: "GT.1", "PR. 107", and "PB.86)". (The U.S. State Department report describes the three major varieties to be AVROS.50, which apparently has been confused with GT.1; PR.107; and PB.36, which is apparently a misprint of PB.86.)

GT.1, originally defoliated 90-100%, has since experienced the greatest amount of branch dieback, and has been the slowest to recover. Branch dieback of 2-3 meters (7-10 feet) or more was quite common. Young trees of this variety and those growing under adverse soil conditions have in many instances died over the past eight months. Latex production in the half year following spraying was reduced by as much as 70-80% in this variety. The current complement of leaves is somewhat abnormal in appearance and the dry rubber content (DRC) of the latex now flowing is subnormal.

PR.107 has turned out to be somewhat less sensitive than GT.1, all of the above described effects having occurred to a somewhat lesser degree. PB.86 was least affected by the herbicides and has now after one growing season recovered to a large extent.

Over-all, the IRCC has determined conservatively that the May to November 1969 latex production of the sprayed rubber trees was reduced by an average of 35-40%. This represents an economic loss so far of approximately U.S. $11.0 million. We judge these figures to be reliable since we were impressed by the detail and accuracy of the records kept by the IRCC and the larger plantations and by the obvious competence and integrity of the professional personnel involved. It should be added that this opinion was shared by the U.S. State Department team that had made the earlier inspection. It is also important to note that the damaged rubber trees in production represent over one-third of all the rubber trees currently in production in Cambodia. Rubber is the first or second most important export commodity of the nation, crucial to its balance of trade.

It is difficult to accurately estimate the entire extent of present and future damage since many direct and indirect factors are involved. Whereas PB.86 may be back to essentially normal production within another year, GT.1 may well level off at only 80% of normal production within another two or three years. Presumably, PR.107 will be intermediate in its rate of recovery. The death of some GT.1 and PR. 107 trees will preclude full recovery of normal production per hectare until their normal time of replacement at about age 40-50. (The larger plantations have trees in blocks of about 100 hectares [250 acres] in all age classes, and follow a regular annual schedule of renewal.)

One of the serious indirect problems that has already resulted from the herbicidal defoliation is the production of a luxuriant understory of weeds throughout the affected area, resulting from greatly increased illumination of the forest floor. These weeds not only compete for the limited soil nutrients and water, but also enormously increase the fire hazard during the dry season. Indeed, we inspected the disastrous results of one 23-hectare (57-acre) fire resulting from just this situation, all the rubber trees having been killed. These weeds are being cut in part, but financial limitations preclude adequate control. The weed-associated losses may well approach the magnitude of the losses resulting from the drop in latex production.

Another problem (which applies most seriously to the many small plantations and to the entirely damaged larger ones) results from the fact that tapping of the injured trees must often be continued almost unabated for pressing financial and social reasons. Most of the families comprising the *ca.* 30,000 inhabitants of the affected area depend upon tapping as their prime source of income. This unfortunate situation prevents the injured trees from recovering as rapidly as they might if they were left alone for a year or two, and is likely to lead to an increased rate of mortality. Moreover, since the tappers are paid on the basis of amount of latex collected daily, they are currently earning minimal wages.

Many of the blocks established during the past several years were decimated regardless of variety, so that the larger plantations in the affected area will largely lack these several age classes. This and the possible need for earlier replacement of mature blocks (owing to possible earlier senility, *i.e.*, earlier drop in latex production) will unbalance the normal rotational cycles for decades to come. An added aggravation is that some of the budwood gardens (the source of the cion material for the reëstablishment of the clonal varieties) were badly damaged.

The dead branch stubs and the weakened condition of the trees may result in future increases in fungal or insect depredations, although there are as yet no indications of this.

Finally, it is of physiological interests to note that a very high proportion of two rubber varieties, TR.1600 and BD.5, have died during the interval since the spraying. It is most fortunate that these two highly sensitive varieties are essentially not in commercial use in the affected area.

Damage to other vegetation. A large variety of garden crops (both agricultural and horticultural) were devastated in the seemingly endless number of small villages scattered throughout the affected area. Virtually all of the *ca.* 30,000 local inhabitants are subsistence farmers that depend for their wellbeing upon their own local produce. These people saw their crops then growing literally wither before their eyes. Indeed, it was the widespread death of the vegetables that heralded the rest of the damage to the area. Their then current crops of vegetables of numerous kinds, of pineapples (*Ananas comosus*), of guavas (*Psidium guajava*), of jack fruit (*Artocarpus integra*), of papayas (*Carica papaya*), and of many, many more were simply destroyed.

Some of the other more important food crops that were largely wiped out at the time included durian (*Durio zibethimus*), manioc (*Manihot esculenta* and *M. ultissima*), tomato (*Lycopersicum esculentum*), several types of beans (*Phaseolus vulgaris, Glycine max, Vigna sesquipedales,* etc.), cauliflower (*Brassica oleracea*), and custard apple (*Annona diversifolia? reticulata?*).

Food plants that seemed to be only little or moderately damaged by the herbicides included taro (*Colocasia esculentum*), ginger (*Zingiber officinale*), banana (*Musa sapietum*, etc.), orange (*Citrus sinensis*), longan (*Nephelium longana*), mango (*Mangifera indica*), sapodilla (*Achras zapota*), sugar palm (*Borassus flabellifera*), and coconut (*Cocos nucifera*). Of these, coconut is now showing a moderate measure of delayed injury not originally expected. A number of annual crops were largely spared because for the most part they had not yet been planted. Rice (*Oryza sativa*), although moderately resistant to the herbicides, falls into this category.

At the time of our visit, the annual plants that had been planted subsequent to the spraying for the most part seemed to be normal in appearance. On the other hand, pineapple plants look healthy but are to date refusing to bear. The new papaya crop is small and the fruits and leaves are somewhat distorted on a number of the plants. Some guava trees have died in the interim, and none of those that have persisted are as yet bearing. The custard apples are for the most part not yet bearing either. Lychee trees (*Litchie chinensis*), apparently not an important crop locally, suffered severe dieback and are not yet bearing. The important jack fruit trees (anticipated by the U.S. State Department team to largely recover) are unfortunately now for the most part dead. Indeed, the dead jack fruit trees stand as grim reminders of the "poison from the sky" beside virtually every home in the area. (The Cambodian Ministry of Agriculture estimates that some 45,000 of these were killed or severely damaged.) The banana plants seem completely normal again and the manioc trees seem to be recovering well (although some of the new fruits are abnormal in shape).

Kapok trees (*Ceiba pentandra*), whose fibers provide a small cash crop for the local inhabitants, were largely killed in village after village. The few surviving trees are not yet bearing their fiber-producing fruits. We inspected two small plantations in the area, one of coffee (*Coffea arabica*) and another of teak (*Tectona grandis*), neither of which seemed to have been damaged by the herbicides.

The forested portions between the plantations and villages in the affected area presently support only a scattering of commercially usable timber trees of a variety of species. Although many of the few tall timber trees had been initially defoliated, most now seem to be slowly recovering (largely through the production of adventitious shoots). We did observe some dead individuals of two commercial species of dipterocarp: lumbor (*Shorea hypochra*) and phdiec (*Anisoptera cochinchinensis*).

Damages to crops other than rubber have been estimated by the Cambodian Ministry of Agriculture to amount to approximately U.S. $1.2 million. The extent of privation caused the local inhabitants cannot be estimated.

Damage to land and soil. We observed no evidence of increased erosion or of soil hardening via laterization and no evidence of change in the level of the water table or of any other physiographic factor. Nor did we find any evidence of weather modification.

Damage to livestock and other animals. All of our interviews with the local inhabitants consistently disclosed that village livestock became ill for a period of several days soon after spraying. Whereas the larger animals (water buffaloes, cattle, and mature pigs and sheep) became only mildly ill and all recovered, some of the smaller ones (chickens, ducks, and young pigs) suffered more severely and in some cases were reported to have died. The domestic mammals were described as having had digestive problems, whereas the domestic birds became partially paralyzed for a time. Apparently many wild birds became similarly disabled and could be captured easily. There were also a number of small dead birds found at the time in the woods and fields.

It is interesting to note here that eastern Cambodia in general has experienced quite a substantial increase in a variety of wildlife, apparently driven out of Vietnam by the defoliation and other ravages of the war. Included are muntjacs and other species of deer, wild cattle (gaurs, bantengs, and some koupreys), elephants, a number of monkey species, and wild pigs.

Effect on humans. Many of the local inhabitants we interviewed spoke of widespread temporary diarrhea and vomiting, particularly among infants and to a lesser extent among the general adult populace. At one location (Chipeang) water was trucked in for a time following spraying to provide uncontaminated water for the children. In those instances where the people depended largely upon deep wells for their water supply we received no report of human digestive problems.

We had a lengthy interview with the physician who directs a hospital in the affected area (at Mimot) that serves some 15,000 people, and which handles about 200 local patients a day. (The doctor speaks not only French and English, but Cambodian and Vietnamese as well.) We also inspected his detailed hospital patient records for 1968 and 1969. This investigation revealed no increase in the incidence of any malady during or subsequent to spraying. Owing to the known abortive and teratogenic effects of 2,4,5-T in laboratory animals and its similar suspected effects amongst the South Vietnamese population, we gave particular attention to this possibility. However, there has been no increase discernible in recent months. (There are about fifty local births per month and the birth of one malformed infant about every two months.)

SOURCE OF THE HERBICIDAL SPRAY

There is, of course, no question that the responsibility for the extensive herbicidal damage we have observed in Cambodia rests upon the United States. Only the United States has the ability and matériel locally to carry out such operations. By its own admission, the United States has in South Vietnam carried out extensive aerial spraying with a variety of herbicides. Indeed, over 10% of the entire surface of South Vietnam has been heavily sprayed over the past eight years. The U.S. State Department report enumerates the spray missions in some detail that were carried out in the neighboring Tay Ninh province of South Vietnam between March and June of 1969.

Some of the Cambodian damage, perhaps as much as one-third of it, certainly appears to be the result of drift from some of these operations. Indeed, such drift is unavoidable given the type of herbicide used, the method of application, and the existing topographical and meteorological conditions.

Although denied by the U.S. Defense Department, the U.S. State Department report concluded that a significant portion of the damage was virtually certain to be the result of direct overflight. We have concluded even less ambiguously that the evidence for direct overflight is incontrovertible. The total amount of damage, the areal extent of damage, the distance of damage from the South Vietnamese operations, the prevailing wind direction during the period in question, and the spatial pattern of severity (in the central portion of the affected area severity essentially the same near the border as 18 kilometers [11 miles] in) have forced us to the conclusion that at least two-thirds of the actual damage in Cambodia was the result of direct overflight. Moreover, a number of the local inhabitants we interviewed reported to have seen spray planes in operation overhead. M. Buoy San, director of the plantation at Chipeang, described to us a low-flying plane spraying his plantation at about 9 a.m. on three separate occasions in April and May.

Some 70,000 hectares (173,000 acres) were at least slightly injured. If one makes the conservative assumption that this entire area was damaged by a dose rate averaging as little as 0.5 kg/hectare (0.4 pound/acre) of active herbicide, a total application of some 35,000 kilograms (77,000 pounds) would have been needed. How much of this could have resulted from drift over the border arising from the U.S. military operations in adjacent South Vietnam?

Each spray plane carries a payload of about 3,600 kilograms (7,900 pounds) of active herbicide. If one can assume that no more than about 10% of the herbicide in each aircraft could have drifted onto the affected area, this would mean that of the order of 100 planes had to have been flying missions rather near to the Cambodian border during April and early May of 1969. Actually (according to the U.S. State Department report) only about half that number of planes flew defoliation missions in the adjacent Tay Ninh province during that time. Moreover, meteorological conditions and other considerations led the U.S. State Department team to conclude that drift could only have originated from five missions apparently totalling 29 planes.

Thus, even assuming a conservative over-all average dose rate of 0.5 kg/hectare (0.4 pound/acre), drift could have accounted for as much as one-third of the total injury that occurred. Our examination of the affected area suggested that its eastern and western portions may have received about 0.5 kg/hectare. However, there is a large central block of perhaps 10,000 hectares (24,700 acres) in which the extent and selectivity of damage suggests a fairly uniform application rate of the order of 2-3 kg/hectare (2-3 pounds/acre). This more heavily damaged zone extends about 20 kilometers (12 miles) from north to south and about 5 kilometers (3 miles) from east to west. It includes the rubber plantations at Dar, Chalang, and Prek Chhlong. The damage on this central block can only be explained on the basis of a direct overflight. It could be accounted for by some seven planes flying at a higher than usual altitude.

We conclude that it is highly likely that the overflights were a deliberate violation of the frontier.* The border is recognizable from the air and both United States air and ground forces seem to be intimately familiar with its location. Although U.S. aircraft violate Cambodian territory daily for purposes of reconnaissance, the daily military combat activities in the region (a number of which we observed

---

* On 18 December 1969, Mr. Thomas R. Pickering, Deputy Director of the Bureau of Politico-Military Affairs of the U.S. Department of State, in testimony before the House Subcommittee on National Security Policy and Scientific Developments (published by the Committee on Foreign Affairs in early 1970) admitted "that the greatest part of the damage was caused by a deliberate and direct overflight of the rubber plantations."

at rather close hand) are for the most part strictly limited to the South Vietnamese side. The fact that rubber plantations (which are readily distinguishable from the air) were so heavily hit (one-third of all of this major Cambodian crop), suggests an attempt at punitive action on the part of the United States. That U.S. pilots are, we are told, under routine standing orders in South Vietnam to avoid the spraying of rubber adds further support to the hypothesis that this particular action was deliberate.

CONCLUSION

Our mission was a sad one, a mission whose raison d'être we wish had never occurred. The loss in rubber production will be relatively easy to ascertain over the next year or two, and restitution will hopefully be made by the United States. (We concur with the U.S. State Department report that a fairly reliable evaluation of damages should be possible following one more growing season, *i.e.*, toward the end of 1970; we concur with the Cambodian Ministry of Agriculture report that an economist should be included in the next visiting team.) The damages to rubber that we have observed are certain to result in a significant setback in Cambodia's slow but promising struggle to strengthen its economy. Therefore, the sooner the United States makes restitution the better.

We feel particularly grieved about the innumerable direct and indirect losses suffered by the innocent local populace. The extent of these losses can never be determined satisfactorily and will never be compensated adequately. We have seen at first hand how particularly drastic this type of military action is for people whose very existence is so closely tied to the land.

Cambodia is a small nation attempting to remain neutral between East and West and to remain at peace with its neighbors despite enormous external pressures from all quarters. We cannot understand and we cannot condone the violations of Cambodian territory by the United States, for which the present report furnishes but one example.

Despite a week of free and unhampered travel by automobile, on foot, and by low-flying aircraft along hundreds of kilometers of the border, we could find no evidence of Viet Cong activity in Cambodia; nor did our repeated conversations with Cambodians and Europeans living along the border suggest any such activity.

We therefore urge that the United States adopt an ironclad policy of respect for the rights of the Khmer people and of the Royal Cambodian Government. Only in this way will we be able to bolster the deteriorating amity between the United States and Cambodia, so important in these times of international disharmony.

Finally, we cannot help but mention the United States herbicidal activities in neighboring South Vietnam. We have witnessed the devastation caused by this relatively minor incursion into Cambodia. How much worse it must be for the hapless peoples of South Vietnam whose lands are being sprayed so much more heavily and systematically. Theirs is a long-term legacy of economic and ecological devastation whose full enormity is difficult to grasp.

Military Use of Herbicides: Some Available Literature

Army, U.S. Dept. of (1969)
EMPLOYMENT OF RIOT CONTROL AGENTS, FLAME, SMOKE, ANTIPLANT AGENTS, AND PERSONNEL DETECTORS IN COUNTERGUERRILLA OPERATIONS.
U.S. Dept. Army Trng. Circ. TC 3-16, 85 pp. (pp. 62-68; 80-81).

Fair, S. D. (1963)
NO PLACE TO HIDE: HOW DEFOLIANTS EXPOSE THE VIET CONG.
Army 14(2):54-55 [also: Armed Forces Chemical Jour. 18(1):5-6.]

House, W. B. et al. (1967)
ASSESSMENT OF ECOLOGICAL EFFECTS OF EXTENSIVE OR REPEATED USE OF HERBICIDES.
U.S. Dept. Defense, DDC AD824314, 369 pp. [the "MRI" report].

Huddle, F. P. (1969)
   TECHNOLOGY ASSESSMENT OF THE VIET-
   NAM DEFOLIANT MATTER: A CASE HISTORY.
   U.S. House Repres., Comm. on Science & Astronau-
   tics, 73 pp.

McCarthy, R. D. (1969)
   ULTIMATE FOLLY: WAR BY PESTILENCE,
   ASPHYXIATION AND DEFOLIATION.
   N. Y.: Knopf, 176 pp. (pp. 74-98).

Mrak, E. M. et al. (1969)
   REPORT OF THE SECRETARY'S COMMISSION
   ON PESTICIDES AND THEIR RELATIONSHIP
   TO ENVIRONMENTAL HEALTH.
   U.S. Dept. Health, Education, & Welfare, 677 pp.

Rose, S. (ed.) (1969)
   CBW: CHEMICAL AND BIOLOGICAL WAR-
   FARE.
   Boston: Beacon, 209 pp. (pp. 62-98).

Scientific Research (1969)
   MISSION TO VIETNAM. [Interview with E. W.
   Pfeiffer & G. H. Orians]
   Scientific Research [†] 4(12):22-30; (13):26-30;
   (15):5.

Tschirley, F. H. (1968)
   RESEARCH REPORT: RESPONSE OF TROPICAL
   AND SUBTROPICAL WOODY PLANTS TO
   CHEMICAL TREATMENTS.
   U.S. Agricultural Research Serv., Publ. CR-13-67,
   197 pp.

Tschirley, F. H. (1969)
   DEFOLIATION IN VIETNAM.
   Science 163:779-786.

Westing, A. H. et al. (1970)
   REPORT ON HERBICIDAL DAMAGE BY THE
   UNITED STATES IN SOUTH-EASTERN CAM-
   BODIA.
   U.S. Congressional Record 116: [in press]

What You Can Do: A Statement and Program
by the Publishers

A Statement by the Publishers

The purpose of the Ballantine/Friends of the Earth Survival Series is to provide the best possible information, written for the intelligent layman, about the principal current threats to the environment that urgently demand remedial action.

We hope to encourage support for the further research that will always be necessary as long as man uses technology and seeks to anticipate the consequences. Proper application of science and humanity will sometimes show that man had better not do what mere technology tells him he can do.

We will also urge action now, based upon what is already known, to prevent using a given technology in advance of assurance that it will not inflict lasting harm.

The coupons below outline a course of remedial action open to the citizen. Advertisements already run by the Sierra Club and by Friends of the Earth have demonstrated the efficacy of the coupon. Citizens who have the time will be able to state their views far better than the coupons do, and we hope people will take the time so to express their views to all or some of the suggested addressees. The trouble you take to use the coupon approach will make a difference. Few men in public life will be so oblivious to citizen views as to ignore the constituency the coupons represent, knowing that their use takes more time than required of people who answer the few telephone questions normally presented in audience-voter rating polls. The use of the coupons can be a first step in citizen participation. The first step can lead to others.

Coupons are fine. Letters are better—letters that reveal the intensity of interest of the writer, letters that show the writer's desire to help the system work far better than it is now working, letters that follow a given controversy through until the proffered solutions make sense and are achieved.

The What You Can Do department of the series is important, but the book is the thing. Each book is intended to fill what has been a gap in publishing. Ordinarily, books take too much lead time to be of current value. We have sped them up so that vital information—the abstract (the contents page and the promotional material), the detailed exposition (the text itself, with such illustrations as are available), and the documentation—can become a readily available part of the concerned citizen's working library. Many magazines require more lead time than these books do, and those that are published on a news-magazine schedule rarely have enough space to provide all the material you may need at hand. And in all but the best organized of homes, magazines have a way of being topped by succeeding issues so rapidly that the lode-bearing strata are lost to all time and to the *Reader's Guide to Periodical Literature*—which is not in many home reference libraries.

We should like to think, further, that the series will be reviewed, interpreted, and enlarged upon in the very media whose limitations we have remarked upon, and nevertheless value very highly for their own unique and indispensable role in letting people know enough about what is happening to their environment to save it in time.

So here is retrievable information for you to put to good use.

IAN BALLANTINE, President
Ballantine Books

DAVID BROWER, President
Friends of the Earth

Muir and Friends

Nearly everybody knows there is an environmental crisis on our space ship. Here is what two new organizations are doing about it, in behalf of the preservation, restoration, and rational use of the ecosphere.

1. The John Muir Institute for Environmental Studies, founded in New Mexico in 1968, is tax deductible. It assumes that the conservationist's cause is good and his heart in the right place, but that he deserves better information. Which is true.

2. Friends of the Earth, founded in New York in 1969, rejoins that the researcher's cause is good, his head in the right place, but that unless we act now on what he already knows, he may never complete his studies. And Friends of the Earth believes it can act adequately only if it is not tax deductible, which it isn't.

Working in tandem, complementing each other, properly separating funds and combining their effort, John Muir Institute and Friends of the Earth can help existing conservation organizations get new things accomplished.

JMI John Muir Institute is conducting a Forum for a Future—biennial symposia in Aspen, Colorado, alternating with conferences in major cities. Participants at the first symposium suggested five routes to equilibrium between man and earth: 1) halt population growth, 2) create *an* ecological ethic that will influence all human affairs, 3) create an economic system not based on growth, and not abusive of the earth, 4) organize voters to demand effective government action, and 5) form new international institutions to deal with the ecological crisis. The 1970 program will concentrate on environmental economics—a symposium and a conference in New York.

John Muir Institute is undertaking to fill in gaps on the research map: 1) independent analysis and 2) critique of major environment-disrupting projects, 3) inquiry into the forces and rates of environmental restoration, 4) certification of fair-conservation practices, and 5) development of ecological conscience in all professions.

And John Muir Institute will prepare illustrated, edited manuscripts for publication, including the international exhibit-format series, The Earth's Wild Places. The series portrays the beauty, diversity, and organic wholeness of life and the natural environment of the planet. This diversity, this wildness, holds answers to questions man has not yet learned how to ask, and it is being obliterated by default. Through creative blending of photographs, prose, and poetry, each book reflects a particular environment and the local culture's view of the relation of man to that environment. Each volume is to appear first in exhibit format for U.S. and European use and later in an inexpensive paperback edition. More than one hundred volumes are envisioned over the next two decades. Preparing the material is JMI's job.

FOE   Friends of the Earth will take it from there, carrying out the publishing operation with McCall Publishing Company and others as necessary. Among the titles scheduled in the series are *Maui and the Wild Kipahulu* by Robert Wenkam and Kenneth Brower (in press); a volume on the Alps by Max Knight and Gerhard Klammet; *A Sense of Place*, by Alan Gussow; a volume on Micronesia by Robert Wenkam and Kenneth Brower; on the Mekong River by John P. Milton and Sterling Seagrave; on the Canadian Rockies by Martin Litton; and on the last great wilderness of the Brooks Range and Arctic Wildlife Range, by John Milton and Kenneth Brower. Books already published (by Ballantine Books) are the *SST and Sonic Boom Handbook* by Professor of Physics William A. Shurcliff and *The Environmental Handbook,* edited for the first national environmental teach-in by Garrett De Bell.

Unhampered by tax-exempt status, Friends of the Earth will also undertake substantial legislative activity, including lobbying and major advertising efforts on critical issues. It will join other conservation organizations in going to court to fight environmental abuse.

FOE's members will be organized into specific task forces that can effectively participate in important battles. The acronym FOE is quite appropriate: friends of the earth must be the foe of whatever or whoever degrades the earth.

LCV   FOE's League of Conservation Voters will mobilize support for political candidates with outstanding conservation records who face close election races. It will not only endorse them, but will also raise money and manpower for their campaigns. The goal is to prove that conservation issues can decide the outcome of an election.

The League of Conservation Voters is strictly nonpartisan and will support candidates from both parties who are truly Friends of the Earth. The League is appraising the candidates for the 1970 congressional elections and raising funds to underwrite its subsequent appeal—that voters channel their political contributions through LCV. We will pass them on undiminished, letting the candidates know that it was concern for the environment that brought them in.

Muir and Friends, Survival Team

Together, John Muir Institute and Friends of the Earth will try to persuade people here and abroad that survival is scientifically and politically feasible.

Both organizations invite—and need—your participation. Both are open for membership, Friends of the Earth starting at $15 (students $5) and John Muir Institute at $50.

Wherever our offices or correspondents are, two hats are worn, two sets of accounts are kept, and one purpose is served—the quest for ways for man to live in reasonable equilibrium with the only life-support system he will be able to use.

It is the evolving, beautiful, stable diversity of living things that makes life possible. Nothing else does, nor will.

JMI MEMBERSHIPS

Regular $50, Supporting $100, Contributing $250,
Life $1,000,* Corporate $1,000.

FOE MEMBERSHIPS

Regular $15, Spouse $5, Student $5, Supporting $25,
Contributing $50, Life $250,* Patron $1,000.*

Life and Patron memberships can be billed quarterly.

FRIENDS OF THE EARTH

☐ I enclose $_____for membership.

☐ I wish to participate actively from time to time.
My special conservation interests are:_____

☐ My own field is:_____

☐ I enclose $_____as a contribution but do not wish to
join now.

NAME _____

ADDRESS _____

CITY _____ STATE _____ ZIP _____

(Contributions to Friends of the Earth are not tax deductible.)

☐ I should like to be kept informed of other books in the
Survival Series.

JOHN MUIR INSTITUTE FOR
ENVIRONMENTAL STUDIES

☐ I enclose $_____for membership.

☐ I enclose $_____as a contribution but do not wish to
join now.

NAME _____

ADDRESS _____

CITY _____ STATE _____ ZIP _____

(Contributions to the John Muir Institute are tax deductible.)

FRIENDS OF THE EARTH
JOHN MUIR INSTITUTE
30 East 42nd Street
New York, N.Y. 10017

The Honorable J. William Fulbright, Chairman
Committee on Foreign Relations
New Senate Office Building
Washington, D. C. 20510

Dear Senator Fulbright:
Mindful as you are of the effects of pollutants that do
not and cannot respect national borders, I request that your
committee investigate the production, and the use in Vietnam, Cambodia, and elsewhere, of the defoliant, 2,4,5-T,
the enormous dangers from which are described in Thomas
Whiteside's book, DEFOLIATION. Will you please let me
know how I may be of assistance in this effort?
                    Sincerely yours,

Name _____

Address _____

City _____ State _____ Zip _____

The Honorable J. William Fulbright, Chairman
Committee on Foreign Relations
New Senate Office Building
Washington, D. C. 20510

The President
The White House
Washington, D. C. 20500

Dear Mr. President:

The enormous dangers implicit in the use of the defoliant, 2,4,5-T, as described in Thomas Whiteside's book, DEFOLIATION, are cause for grave apprehension, and I am sure they trouble the majority of informed citizens in the United States and in other nations. I share the belief you have expressed that we must now or never take steps to halt environmental degradation, and I believe that the 2,4,5-T may be one of the most devastating pollutants of all. I am alarmed, further, at the difficulties Mr. Whiteside experienced in obtaining from the government the facts of the defoliation crisis that are essential to an intelligent participation by the citizen in his government.

What role would you suggest I myself play to be of service in ending the pollution of the environment and of information that the defoliation story reveals?

Sincerely yours,

Name _____

Address _____

City _____ State _____ Zip _____

The President
The White House
Washington, D. C. 20500

The Honorable Philip A. Hart, Chairman
Subcommittee on Energy, Natural Resources, and Environment
Senate Office Building
Washington, D. C. 20510

Dear Senator Hart:

Thank you for your leadership in undertaking to investigate the hazards in the widespread use in Vietnam, Cambodia, and in the United States, of the defoliant 2,4,5-T and the accompanying contaminant, dioxin, hazards revealed in Thomas Whiteside's book, DEFOLIATION. I am sure you realize the difficulty and importance of looking under the camouflage and revealing the truth, furthering Mr. Whiteside's excellent investigative efforts. Will you please let me know if I can assist the committee's work in any way?

                              Sincerely yours,

Name _____

Address _____

City_____ State _____ Zip _____

The Honorable Philip A. Hart, Chairman
Subcommittee on Energy, Natural Resources, and Environment
Senate Office Building
Washington, D. C. 20510

The Honorable U Thant
Secretary-General
United Nations
New York, N. Y.

Dear Mr. Thant:

In view of the meetings to be held by the United Nations in 1972 to consider pollution of the biosphere, I hope you will find means to give careful consideration to the immediate and long-range effects of the defoliant, 2,4,5-T, and the accompanying contaminant, dioxin, as described by Thomas Whiteside in his book, DEFOLIATION. This would seem to be a subject warranting concurrent consideration by the World Health Organization, the Food and Agricultural Organization, and the Director of Science and Technology. It would appear to be of vital importance for the world to understand fully, in undertaking "The Green Revolution", the hazard to man himself when he attempts, through chemical means, to make the chemicals of life unavailable to other forms of life. It will serve mankind poorly to produce more food at the expense of destroying parts of the ecosystem that impair the continuity of life, including those life forms that we directly or indirectly depend upon for sustenance.

Sincerely yours,

Name _____

Address _____

City_____ State _____ Zip_____

The Honorable U Thant
Secretary-General
United Nations
New York, N. Y.

The Honorable Robert S. McNamara, President
The World Bank
1818 H Street, N.W.
Washington, D. C. 20006

Dr. Matthew Meselson, Chairman
AAAS Herbicide Assessment Commission
American Association for the Advancement of Science
Biological Laboratories
Harvard University
Cambridge, Mass.

The Honorable Robert S. McNamara, President
The World Bank
1818 H Street, N.W.
Washington, D. C. 20006

Dear Mr. McNamara:

In view of the alarming indications of teratogenic effects of the defoliant 2,4,5-T and the accompanying contamination of dioxin revealed in the Thomas Whiteside book, DEFOLIATION, could you let me know what steps the World Bank may be able to take, pending the research that can guarantee the absence of such contamination in defoliants, to prohibit the use of 2,4,5-T in any programs receiving assistance from the World Bank?

Sincerely yours,

Name _____

Address _____

City _____ State _____ Zip _____

- -

Dr. Matthew Meselson, Chairman
AAAS Herbicide Assessment Commission
American Association for the Advancement of Science
Biological Laboratories
Harvard University
Cambridge, Mass.

Dear Dr. Meselson:

I should like to express my appreciation for the work you are undertaking with respect to the potential teratogenic hazards of 2,4,5-T and the accompanying contaminant, dioxin, described in Thomas Whiteside's book, DEFOLIATION. I should appreciate being kept informed of the progress of your studies.

Sincerely yours,

Name _____

Address _____

City _____ State _____ Zip _____

Mr. Ralph Nader
Center for the Study of Responsive Law
1908 Q Street, N.W.
Washington, D. C. 20009

Dear Mr. Nader:

Thank you for your contribution toward revealing the hazards to the total environment posed by the defoliant 2,4,5-T and the accompanying contaminant, dioxin, as described in Thomas Whiteside's book, DEFOLIATION. Would you please let me know if there is anything I can do to further your investigations in behalf of the public.

Sincerely yours,

Name _____

Address _____

City _____ State _____ Zip _____

- -

Dr. Gerardo Bodowski, Director-General
International Union for the Conservation of Nature
1110 Morges, Switzerland

Dear Dr. Bodowski:

In the course of the IUCN Program for rational use of the biosphere, I hope you will give careful consideration to the immediate and long-range effects of the defoliant 2,4,5-T and the accompanying contaminant, dioxin, as described by Thomas Whiteside in his book, DEFOLIATION. It would seem to be of great importance to undertake thorough research on the side effects, on human beings as well as on the land mechanism itself, of continued use of such potentially disastrous means as chemical defoliation in the attempts to increase—or deny—the production of food.

Will you let me know what ways there are through which I may assist the IUCN in this work?

Sincerely yours,

Name _____

Address _____

City _____ State _____ Zip _____

Mr. Ralph Nader
Center for the Study of Responsive Law
1908 Q Street, N.W.
Washington, D. C. 20009

Dr. Gerardo Bodowski, Director-General
International Union for the Conservation of Nature
1110 Morges, Switzerland

The Honorable Walter J. Hickel
Secretary of the Interior
Washington, D. C.

The Honorable John C. Stennis, Chairman
Committee on Armed Services
Senate Office Building
Washington, D. C. 20510

The Honorable Walter J. Hickel
Secretary of the Interior
Washington, D. C.

Dear Mr. Hickel:

In view of your responsibilities concerning pollution of the waters of the United States and its territories, and in view further of the pervasiveness of the pollution resulting from oil spills on the oceans of the world, and in our own coastal and estuarine waters and your grave concern about this, I hope you will also investigate fully the further hazard to our waters from the use of the defoliant 2,4,5-T and the accompanying contaminant, dioxin, as described by Thomas Whiteside in his book, DEFOLIATION.

Will you please let me know in what way I may assist this effort?

Sincerely yours,

Name_____

Address_____

City_____ State _____ Zip_____

The Honorable John C. Stennis, Chairman
Committee on Armed Services
Senate Office Building
Washington, D. C. 20510

Dear Senator Stennis:

Mindful as you are of the effects of pollutants that do not and cannot respect national borders, I request that your committee investigate the production, and the use in Vietnam, Cambodia, and elsewhere, of the defoliant, 2,4,5-T, the enormous dangers from which are described in Thomas Whiteside's book, DEFOLIATION. Will you please let me know how I may be of assistance in this effort?

Sincerely yours,

Name_____

Address_____

City_____ State _____ Zip_____

The Honorable John C. Stennis, Chairman
Committee on Armed Services
Senate Office Building
Washington, D. C. 20510

Dear Senator Stennis:

   same as for Senator Fulbright

The Honorable Melvin R. Laird
Secretary of Defense
Washington, D. C.

Dear Mr. Laird:

   The book by Thomas Whiteside, DEFOLIATION, raises
vital questions concerning not only the pervasiveness of pollution resulting from the application of the defoliant, 2,4,5-
T in operations in Vietnam and elsewhere, but also the relationship of this use to the Geneva convention on chemical
and bacteriological warfare. The announcement by Dr.
DuBridge that your department would restrict the use of
2,4,5-T to areas remote from the population in Vietnam
to assure public safety pending further research has not
been, apparently, carried out.
   In view of the President's antipollution program, can you
clarify the position of the Department of Defense?

                              Sincerely yours,
                                        etc.

March of Dimes
315 Park Avenue South
New York, N. Y.
Gentlemen:
   I am pleased to support your program to minimize birth
defects in the human population and wish to continue. In
view of the alarming indications of teratogenic effects of
the defoliant 2,4,5-T revealed in the Thomas Whiteside
book, DEFOLIATION, could you tell me what your plans
are for research on the effects of 2,4,5-T and the accompanying contamination of dioxin upon the human embryo?

                              Sincerely,
                                        etc.

The Honorable Melvin R. Laird
Secretary of Defense
Washington, D. C.

March of Dimes
315 Park Avenue South
New York, New York

INDEX

Abrams, Creighton Williams, Jr., commander U.S. Military Assistance Command, Vietnam, 90

Agriculture, Department of, 5 ff.

alpha-naphthol, 62, 67

American Association for the Advancement of Science, 18

resolution on herbicides, 99

anemia, 8

antiplant agents: *see* herbicides; also Army Training Circular TV 3-16, 73

application of herbicides, 73 ff.

Army Training Circular TC 3-16, 73 ff.

arsenic: *see* cacodylic acid

bamboo, xiv, 14, 90

base camp defense, 87

Bates, Richard, 19

beans, damaged by 2,4,5-T, 125

beriberi, 8

Bien Hoa, Vietnam, 7, 32

biological warfare, x, 3, 34

defined, 35

President Nixon's statement, 34, 96-97

Bionetics Research Laboratories (Litton Industries subsidiary), 16 ff.

report (selections), 69 ff.

birth control regulators, 46

birth defects: *see* teratogenic properties

Blue, Agent, 6, 75-76

composition, 84

use rate, 84

Boi Loi Woods, 51

Bonnet, Henri, xii

Bromacil, 77

composition, 84

Brucker, Wilbur M., Secretary of the Army, x

butyl ester 2,4-D: *see* 2,4-D

cacodylic acid, 7, 75, 76

effect on rice, 108

Cambodia, 14-15, 117 ff.

Camp Detrick: *see* Fort Detrick

cancer: *see* carcinogenic properties

Captan, 58, 62

Carbaryl, 58, 62

carcinogenic properties, 18

cauliflower damage, 126

chemical warfare, x, 3, 34

Pres. Nixon statement, 96

chicks, 38, 46

Children's Cancer Research Foundation, 19

chloracne, 37, 48

Christian Science Monitor, 9

cleft palate, 61

coconut damage, 126

Commission on Pesticides and Their Relationship to Environmental Health (HEW), 18

Report, 57 ff.

compensation, 15

concealment, 73

contraception: *see* birth control regulators

Crimes Against Humanity, xvi

Crops Protection Research Branch, Dept. of Agriculture, 14

CS, x

custard apple damage, 126

cyclamates, 46

cystic kidney, 61 ff.

DDT, 7

Defense, United States Dept. of, 19 ff., 23, 44 ff.

defoliation

agents: *see* herbicides

beginnings, 1-6

extent, 2, 3, 85

mission review, 9

purposes, 1, 73, 87 ff.

technique, 73-84

deformities, 16 ff.

see also teratogenic properties

*A powerful, provocative book
for those who care about
what tomorrow might bring . . .*

Moment in the Sun

Robert and Leona Train Rienow

A report on the Deteriorating Quality of the American Environment

"A VERY IMPORTANT BOOK . . . We've been told for some years now that the wide open spaces are getting narrower all the time, and quicker than some of us might think. The authors of this book lay it right on the line . . . after reading this sane and humane book, one wants to plead with everybody to keep aware, and not regard these things as part of some inevitable black comedy."

—*Harper's Magazine*

A Sierra Club-Ballantine Book   95¢

To order by mail, enclose price of book plus 5¢ a copy for handling and send to Dept. CS, Ballantine Books, 36 West 20th Street, New York, N.Y. 10003.

SURVIVAL IN THE SEVENTIES DEPENDS UPON YOUR BEING INFORMED

Here is your Survival Kit:

THE ENVIRONMENTAL HANDBOOK: Prepared for the First National Environmental Teach-In, edited by Garrett De Bell
> *A Ballantine/Friends of the Earth Book—95¢*

CHEMICAL AND BACTERIOLOGICAL (BIOLOGICAL) WEAPONS AND THE EFFECTS OF THEIR POSSIBLE USE, a United Nations Report, with a special Foreword by George Wald, Department of Biology, Harvard University
> *A Ballantine Walden Edition—$1.25*

PERILS OF THE PEACEFUL ATOM: The Myth of Safe Nuclear Power Plants, by Richard Curtis and Elizabeth Hogan
> *A Ballantine Walden Edition—$1.25*

S/S/T AND SONIC BOOM HANDBOOK, by William A. Shurcliff
> *A Ballantine/Friends of the Earth Book—95¢*

MOMENT IN THE SUN, by Robert and Leona Train Rienow
> *A Sierra Club/Ballantine Book—95¢*

THE FRAIL OCEAN, by Wesley Marx
> *A Sierra Club/Ballantine Book—95¢*

THE POPULATION BOMB, by Dr. Paul Ehrlich
A Sierra Club/Ballantine Book—95¢

DEFOLIATION, What Are Our Herbicides Doing to
Us?, by Thomas Whiteside, Foreword by George Wald
A Ballantine/Friends of the Earth Book—95¢

What Else Can You Do?

Contact:

FRIENDS OF THE EARTH, 30 East 42nd Street, New
York, N.Y. 10017

THE SIERRA CLUB, 1050 Mills Tower, San Francisco,
California 94104. The Sierra Club, founded in 1892 by
John Muir and one of the nation's oldest, largest, and
most active conservation organizations, invites participation in its program.

ZERO POPULATION GROWTH, 367 State Street, Los
Altos, California 94002

NATIONAL AUDUBON SOCIETY, 1130 5th Avenue,
New York, N.Y. 10028

To order survival books by mail, send price of book plus 5¢ for
postage for each to Ballantine Books, Inc., 36 West 20th St.,
New York, N.Y. 10003

THE MOST IMPORTANT BOOK
OF THE NEW DECADE

1970's—THE LAST CHANCE FOR A
FUTURE THAT MAKES ECOLOGICAL SENSE

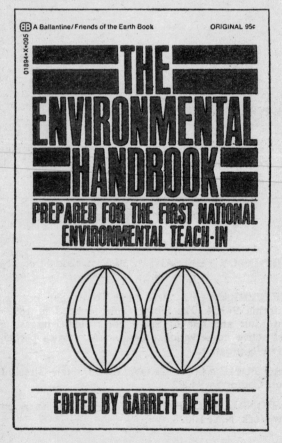

BB A Ballantine/Friends of the Earth Book

ORIGINAL 95¢

01894-X-095

THE
ENVIRONMENTAL
HANDBOOK

PREPARED FOR THE FIRST NATIONAL
ENVIRONMENTAL TEACH-IN

EDITED BY GARRETT DE BELL